JOURNEYS

Reader's Notebook

Volume 2

Grade 1

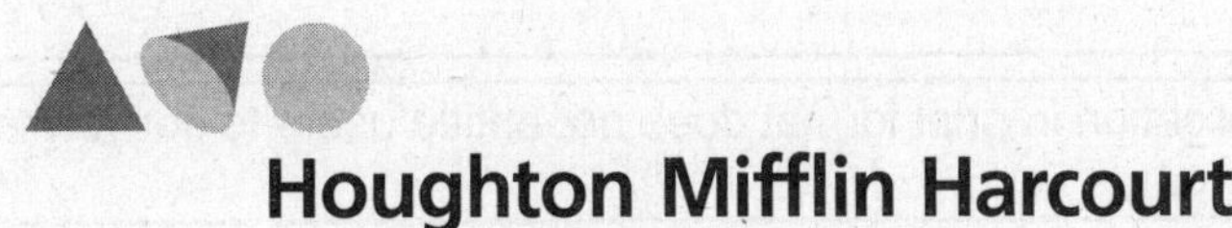

Printed in the U.S.A.

ISBN 978-0-544-59260-5

24 0928 23 22 21

4500821213 C D E F G

Contents

Unit 4

Unit 5

Unit 6

Name ________________________________

Words with Long *o*

Let's Go to the Moon!
Phonics: Words with Long *o*

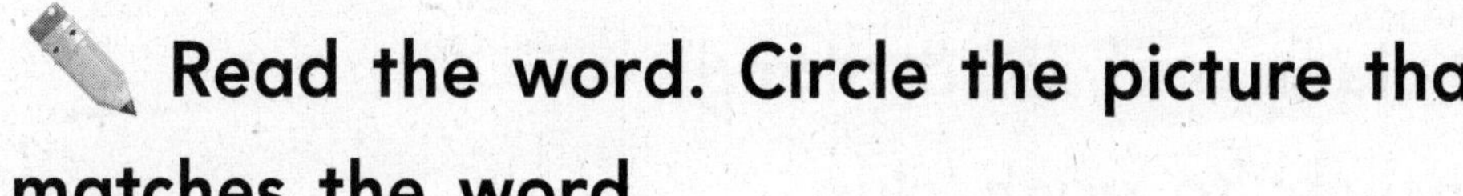

Read the word. Circle the picture that matches the word.

1. home

2. go

3. stone

4. robe

5. hole

Name ______________________________

Words to Know

Listen to the clues and read along.
Circle the best answer to each clue.

1. This means **in a circle.**	**around**	**think**
2. This means **not heavy.**	**because**	**light**
3. You do this to let people look at something.	**bring**	**show**
4. After is its opposite.	**before**	**carry**
5. You do this with bags.	**carry**	**because**
6. This tells why.	**because**	**around**
7. Take away is its opposite.	**light**	**bring**
8. Your brain does this.	**think**	**before**

Name ____________________

Let's Go to the Moon!
Phonics: Words with Long *o*

Words with Long *o*

Look at the picture. Name each picture.
Write the missing letters to complete the word.

1.
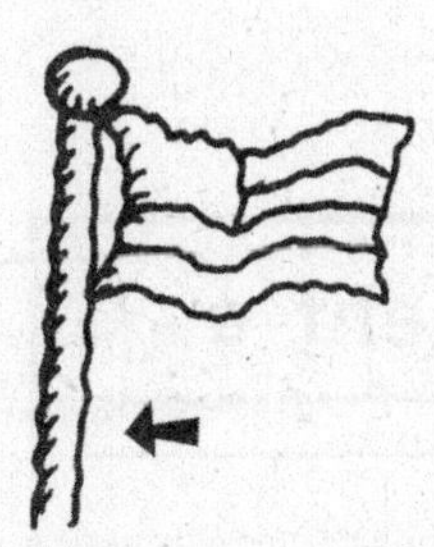

p ___ l ___

2.
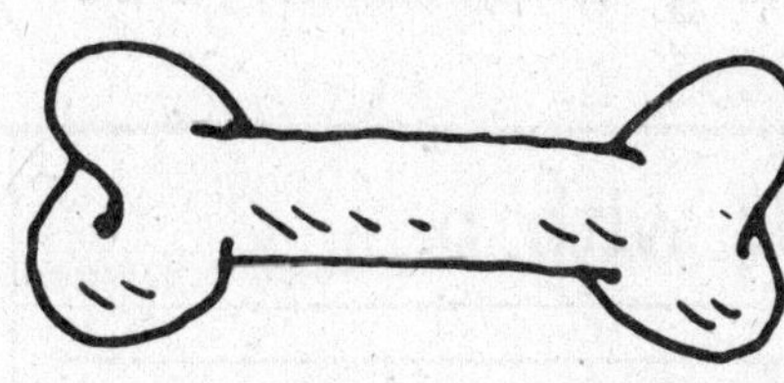

b ___ n ___

3.

g ___

4.
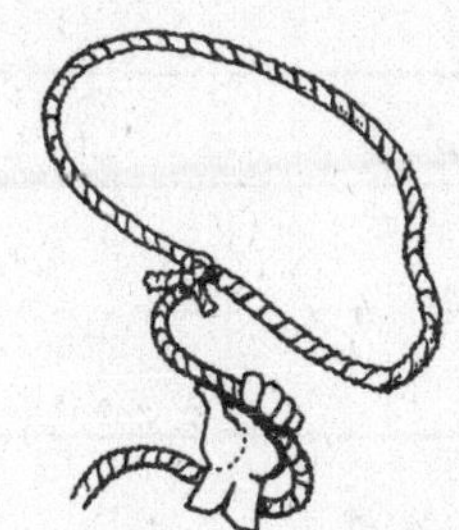

r ___ p ___

5.

s t ___ v ___

6.
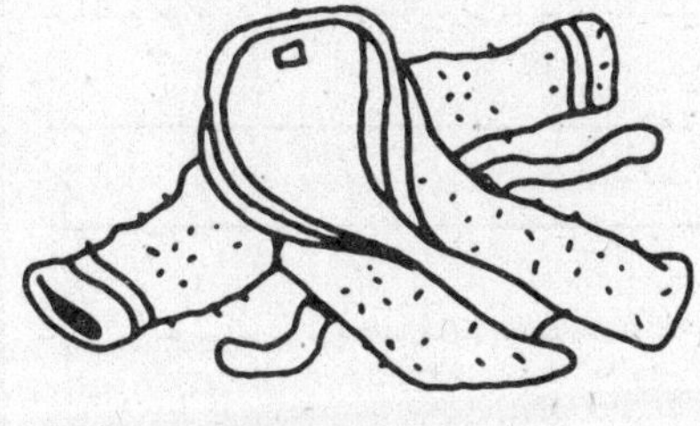

r ___ b ___

Name ____________________

Spelling Words with the Long *o* Sound

Sort the words. Write the correct Spelling Words in each column.

Ends with o	Ends with Silent e

Spelling Words

so
go
home
hole
no
rope
joke
bone
stove
poke

Name ____________________

What Is a Question?

Circle each question.

1. What did you see?

2. Can you look up?

3. Is that the sun?

4. I think I will read.

5. Where did Mike go?

6. They are at the game.

7. How many rocks does Liz have?

8. I like to tell jokes.

Choose one question. Add details.

____

____

Name ______________________

Using Details

 **Draw a picture of something you discovered, or found.**

Write sentences about when you saw your discovery.

One day I **found** a ______________________.

When I **saw** it, I ______________________.

Then I ______________________.

Main Idea

All my sentences tell about ______________________.

Name ___________________________________

Words with Long *u*

Let's Go to the Moon!
Phonics: Words with Long *u*

Circle the word that names the picture.

1.

flute flat

2.

mole mule

3.

hang huge

4.

cute cut

5.

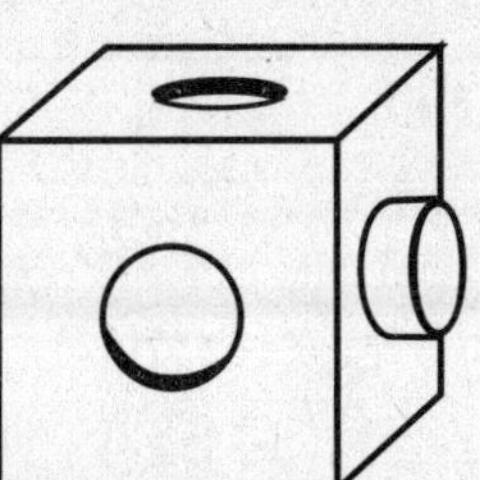

cone cube

Name ______________________ Date ______

Let's Go to the Moon!

Interview an Astronaut

Today you are a reporter. A reporter asks a person questions and writes down the answers. Read pages 20–23. Think about what you read. Then write a question you would like to ask an astronaut. Then pretend to be the astronaut. Write the answer.

Q: ______________________

____

A: ______________________

____

Name ______________________ Date ______

Let's Go to the Moon!
Independent Reading

Read pages 28–33. Think about what you read. Write a question you would like to ask an astronaut. Then pretend to be the astronaut. Write your answer.

Q:

A:

Name ______________________________

Let's Go to the Moon!
Spelling: Words with Long *o*

Spelling Words with the Long *o* Sound

Spelling Words

- so
- go
- home
- hole
- no
- rope
- joke
- bone
- stove
- poke

Write the Spelling Words that rhyme with **woke.**

1. ______________ **2.** ______________

Write the Spelling Words that begin with **h.**

3. ______________ **4.** ______________

Write the Spelling Words that rhyme with **Jo.**

5. ______________

6. ______________

7. ______________

Name ______________________

Writing Questions

Write the correct word from the Word Bank to begin each sentence. Write the correct end mark.

Word Bank

What	Can	When	Where	Do	Are

1. ______________ can I put my hat ___

2. ______________ can they see ___

3. ______________ you see me ___

4. ______________ you need a snack ___

5. ______________ you cold ___

6. ______________ do you go ___

Name ____________________

Let's Go to the Moon!
Writing: Narrative Writing

Planning My Sentences

 **Draw and write details that tell what happened.**

My Topic: ____________________

First Detail

Second Detail

Last Detail

Name ___

Let's Go to the Moon!
Spelling: Words with Long *o*

Spelling Words with the Long *o* Sound

Spelling Words

so
go
home
hole
no
rope
joke
bone
stove
poke

Write a Spelling Word to complete each sentence.

1. The pot on the ___ is hot.

2. Can you wrap the ___ around the pole?

3. What ___ does a fox live in?

4. I can tell a funny ___ .

5. Stand up ___ that I can see you.

6. It is time to ___ to bed.

Name ______

Spiral Review

Circle each proper noun. Some of them have two words in their name. Then write the proper noun correctly.

1. My friend mel has a box of gem stones.
2. We live in oak lane.
3. She has a cat named red.
4. I saw the dog show.

Draw a line under each title. Then write the titles and names correctly.

5. Mom's friend is mrs. Dell.
6. Will dr. Wade visit the class?

Name ___________________________

Grammar in Writing

A sentence that asks something is called a **question.** A question begins with a capital letter and ends with a **question mark.**

Fix the mistakes in these sentences. Use proofreading marks.

Examples: does the moon have plants ?
Is the moon dusty. ?

1. Did you know his name
2. when did they go?
3. Why do you have your bike.
4. what do cats eat?
5. is the Moon hot or cold.

Proofreading Marks	
∧	Add
≡	Capital letter

Name ____________________

Words with Long *e*

The Big Trip
Phonics: Words with Long *e*

 Circle the word that matches the picture.

1.

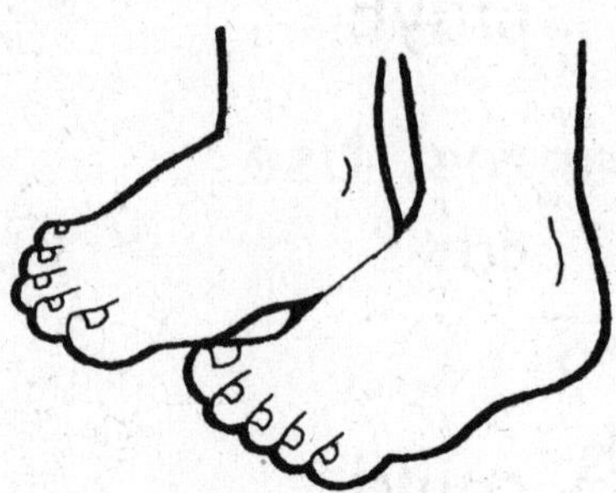

feel feet

2.

tree tea

3.

me he

4.

leaf leap

5.

seat street

6.

see bee

Name ______________________________

Words to Know

Listen to the questions. Read along. Circle the best answer to each question.

1. What word goes with **might?**	maybe	there
2. What word goes with **do not?**	car	don't
3. What word goes with **true?**	could	sure
4. What word goes with **drive?**	car	there
5. What word goes with **here?**	there	don't
6. What word goes with **can?**	cart	could
7. What word comes after the words **"This story is ______"?**	don't	about
8. What word tells how you travel?	by	maybe

Name ___

Words with Long *e*

 **Circle the word that completes the sentence.**

1. I can ___ you how to plant seeds.

teach **beach**

2. These are big ___ .

bees **seeds**

3. I will put them in ___ holes.

jeep **deep**

4. Help me ___ my watering can.

reach **peach**

5. Before long, we will see a small ___ .

beef **leaf**

Name ______________________________

Spelling Words with the Long *e* Sound

Sort the words. Write the correct Spelling Words in each column.

Words with e	Words with ea	Words with ee

Word with Silent e

____

Spelling Words

- me
- be
- read
- feet
- tree
- keep
- eat
- mean
- sea
- these

Name ______________________________

Compound Sentences

Draw a line under the correct compound sentence in each pair.

1. Max took the bus, and we walked.

   Max took the bus and we walked.

2. Do you know, or should I tell you.

   Do you know, or should I tell you?

3. Work quickly, but be careful.

   Work quickly, but be careful?

Write the correct end mark to finish each compound sentence.

4. Stay in line, and wait for the bell ____

5. Is your sister here, or is she at home ____

Name ______________________________

Details for Where and When

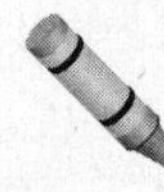

Draw a picture of something you saw or did on a trip.

Write sentences about your trip.

Who	Action	Where

Who	Action	When

Who	Action	Where

Name ______________________________

Words Ending with *ng, nk*

Circle the letters that finish the word.
Write the word.

1.

ba____

(nk, ng)

____

2.

dri____

(nk, ng)

____

3.

swi____

(nk, ng)

____

4.

ki____

(nk, ng)

____

Name ______________________ Date ______

The Big Trip

Travel Riddles

Let's have fun with riddles about **The Big Trip**! Read the clues and the question. Write the answer in a sentence.

I have two wheels. I am pulled by an animal. What am I? ***Do you need a clue? Read pages 60–61.***

____.

I have no wheels. You can ride in my basket. I go in the air. What am I? ***Do you need a clue? Read pages 64–65.***

____.

I have four wheels. You can put your suitcase on top of me. What am I? ***Do you need a clue? Read pages 56–57.***

____.

Name ______________________ Date ______

Now you write a travel riddle! After you write your riddle, share it with a friend. A riddle gives clues. You write the clues. Then a riddle asks a question. The question is already written. You write the answer. Do not let your friend see it! Write the pages from **The Big Trip** where your reader can find clues.

Clues: ______________________

What kind of travel am I? ______________________

Do you need a clue? Read pages: ______________________

Name ______________________

Spelling Words with the Long *e* Sound

Write the Spelling Word that names each picture.

Spelling Words

- me
- be
- read
- feet
- tree
- keep
- eat
- mean
- sea
- these

1. ______________

2. ______________

3. ______________

4. ______________

5. ______________

6. ______________

Writing Compound Sentences

Write a compound sentence by combining each pair of shorter sentences.

1. Are you ready? Should I wait?

or

2. Walk the dog. Feed the cat.

and

3. I feel good. Joe is sick.

but

Name ____________________

Planning My Sentences

Draw and write details that tell what happened first, next, and last.

My Topic: ____________________

First

Next

Last

Name ______________________

Spelling Words with the Long *e* Sound

The Big Trip
Spelling: Words with Long *e*

Write a Spelling Word from the box to complete each sentence.

Spelling Words

me
be
read
feet
tree
keep
eat
mean
sea
these

1. Look at the leaves on that ______________.

2. What do you ______________ in your backpack?

3. I like to swim in the ______________.

4. Pick from ______________ games.

5. A duck has two ______________.

6. Will you ______________ to me?

Name ____________________

Spiral Review

Draw a line under each command.

1. We watched the game.
2. Watch where you walk.
3. Be kind to the animals.
4. What kind of dog is that?

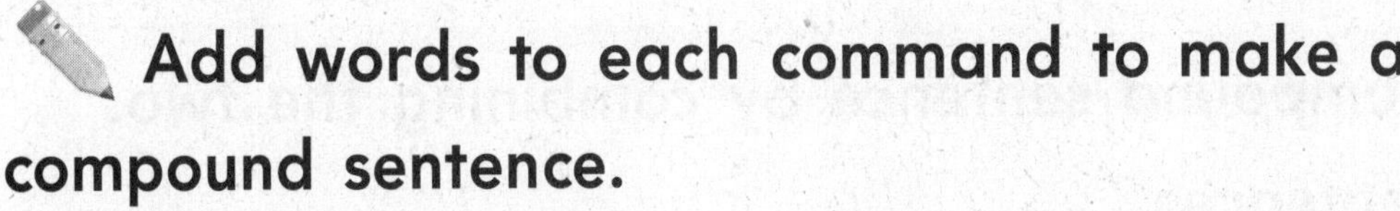

Add words to each command to make a compound sentence.

5. Wait for your turn.

____

____

6. Listen carefully.

____

____

Name ___________________________

Grammar in Writing

The Big Trip
Grammar: Compound Sentences

A **compound sentence** is made up of two shorter sentences joined by a comma and **and, but**, or **or.**

Underline each compound sentence.

1. The girls walked or rode the bus to school.

2. Mom drives to work, but Dad takes a train.

3. Is the game today, or is it tomorrow?

Write a compound sentence by combining the two shorter sentences.

4. Take a nap. Don't be late.

______________________________ but

____

5. I have paper. Larry has pencils.

______________________________ and

____

Name ______________________________

Words with *ai*, *ay*

Read the words. Circle the word that names the picture. Then write the word.

1.

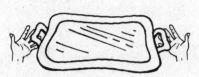

tray ray

____

2.

sail nail

____

3.

hay day

____

4.

paint pain

____

5.

train rain

____

Name ________________________________

Words to Know

Circle the correct word to complete each sentence.

1. Fran ate her beets (these, first).

2. Beets are planted in the (ground, sometimes).

3. (Food, Sometimes) Fran eats salad, too.

4. Fran has to eat all the (food, your) on her plate.

5. "Eat (ground, your) peas," said Mom.

6. The peas are (your, right) from the shop.

7. Fran looked (under, first) her peas.

8. Fran said, "(These, Under) peas look good!"

Name ____________________

Words with *ai*, *ay*

Read the words. Circle the word that names the picture.

1. 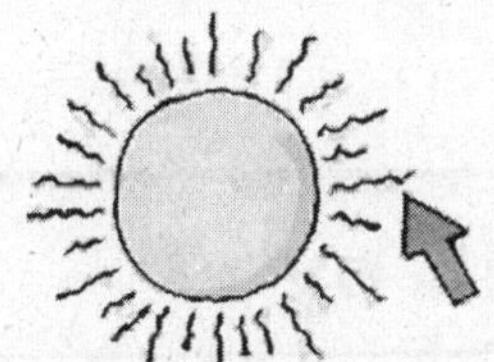 tray ray

2.  sail tail

3.  may play

4.  rain main

5.  paint pant

Name ______________________________

Spelling Words with the Vowel Pairs *ai*, *ay*

Sort the words. Write the correct Spelling Words in each column.

Words with ai	Words with ay

Spelling Words

play
grain
sail
mail
may
rain
way
day
stay
pain

Name ______________________

Where Does Food Come From?
Names of Months, Days, and Holidays

Months, Days, and Holidays

Listen to the names in the Word Bank. Read along. Circle the month, day, or holiday in each sentence. Write it correctly on the line.

Word Bank

Labor Day	Tuesday	May	June	Saturday	August

1. On labor day we had a picnic. ______________

2. On tuesday Hank makes a cake. ______________

3. We plant seeds each may. ______________

Draw a line under the correct sentence in each pair.

4. Ike likes June for planting beans.
Ike likes june for planting beans.

5. I picked beans on Saturday.
I picked beans on saturday.

6. Peaches grow best in august.
Peaches grow best in August.

Name ______________________

Using Different Kinds of Sentences

Where Does Food Come From?
Writing: Narrative Writing

Write a friendly letter about a special meal you had. Write statements and a question.

20

Dear ______________,

I ate ______________ with ______________.

____.

(statement)

____.

(statement)

____?

(question)

______________,

Name ______________________________

Contractions *'ll, 'd*

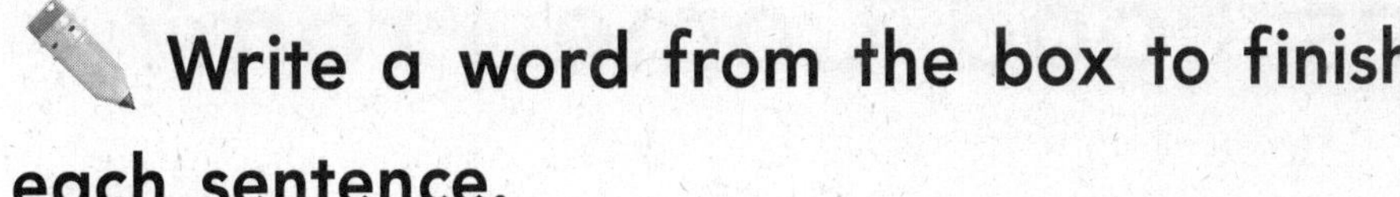

Write a word from the box to finish each sentence.

I'd

he'd	**she'll**	**I'd**	**they'll**	**we'd**

1. Ben said that ____________ be late today.

2. Beth said ____________ go to the beach.

3. Mom and Dad said ____________ go out at five.

4. Gus said, "____________ like to play in the sand."

5. We think ____________ like a day at the beach.

Name ______________________ Date ______

Where Does Food Come From?

Make a Meal!

I am going to have a glass of milk and a grilled cheese sandwich with tomatoes for lunch. I need four different kinds of food. Write where each food comes from. Look at pages 98–99, 104–105, and 107 for text evidence to help you.

1. Milk comes from ______________________.

2. Bread comes from ______________________.

3. Cheese comes from ______________________.

4. Tomatoes come from ______________________.

Name ______________________ Date ______

Now it's time for breakfast! Draw foods on the plate. Label them. Write a sentence telling where each food comes from. Look in the selection for text evidence to help you.

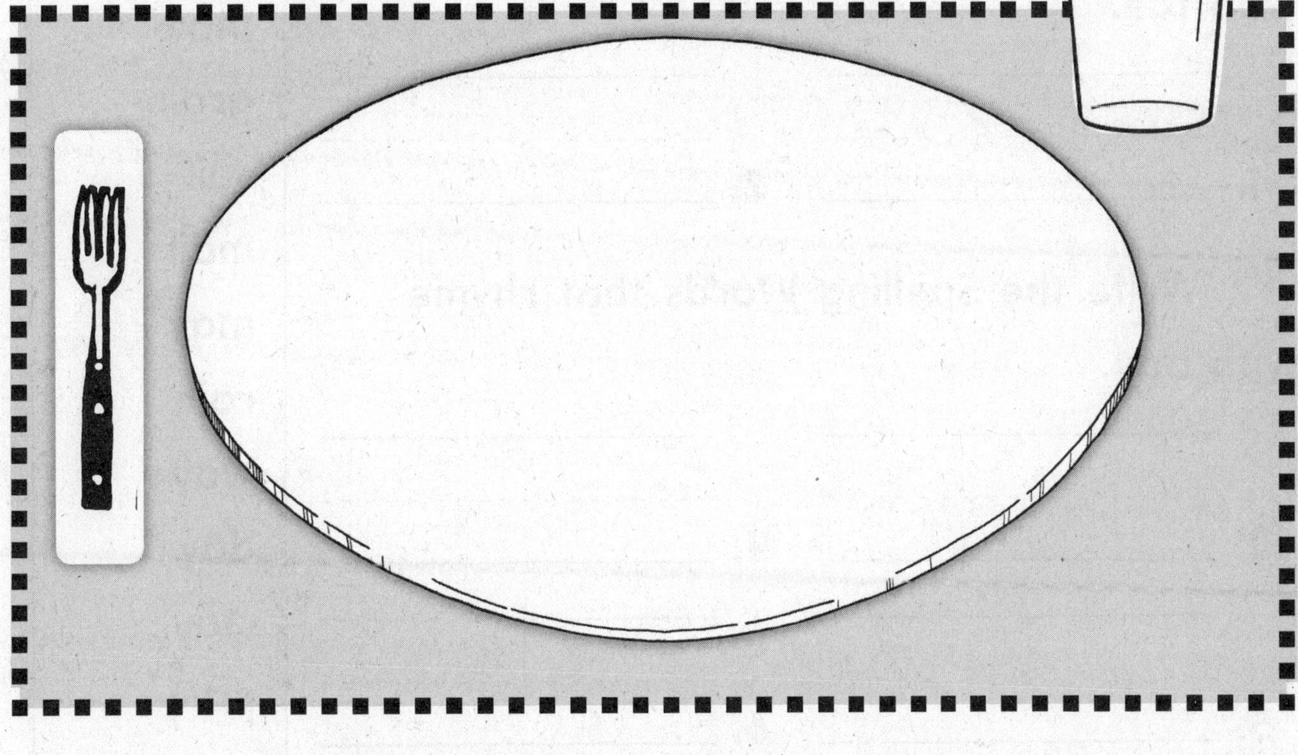

Name ______________________________

Where Does Food Come From?
Spelling: Words with *ai, ay*

Spelling Words with the Vowel Pairs *ai*, *ay*

Spelling Words

- play
- grain
- sail
- mail
- may
- rain
- way
- day
- stay
- pain

Write the Spelling Words that rhyme with **fail.**

1. ______________ 2. ______________

Write the Spelling Words that rhyme with **bay.**

3. ______________ 4. ______________

5. ______________ 6. ______________

7. ______________

Write the Spelling Words that rhyme with **main.**

8. ______________ 9. ______________ 10. ______________

Name ____________________

Commas in Dates

Circle the comma in each date.

1. Ms. Ray moved to the farm on October 25, 2016.
2. She planted wheat on March 13, 2017.
3. She got some chicks on May 28, 2017.
4. She had eggs for sale on June 4, 2018.

The date in each sentence is underlined. Write the date correctly.

5. This patch was planted on <u>march 16 2018</u>.

____

6. The peas were planted on <u>april 23 2018</u>.

____

Name ______________________________

Planning My Letter

 Write and draw details that tell what happened first, next, and last.

I will write my letter to ______________________________.

I will tell about ______________________________.

First

Next

Last

Name ______________________________

Spelling Words with the Long *a* Sound

Write the correct word to complete each sentence.

1. Can you come out and ______________ ?

play **clay**

2. In April there is a lot of ______________ .

rake **rain**

3. Let us ______________ on the lake.

sail **tail**

4. I feel a ______________ in my leg.

train **pain**

5. Wheat is a ______________ .

grain **green**

Name ______________________

Spiral Review

 **Circle the correct verb. Then write the sentence with the correct verb.**

1. The kids (walk, walks) around the pond.

____

2. Nine sheep (eat, eats) the grass.

____

3. Ducks (flap, flaps) their wings.

____

4. One mule (sleep, sleeps) in the hay.

____

5. Pigs (play, plays) in the mud.

____

Name ________________________________

Grammar in Writing

Where Does Food Come From?
Grammar: Names of Months, Days and Holidays

The name of each **month, day,** and **holiday** begins with a capital letter. When you write a date, use a **comma** between the day of the month and the year.

Example:
labor day is monday september 7 2018.

Listen to the names of months and holidays in the Word Bank. Read along. Fix the mistakes in these sentences. Use proofreading marks.

Word Bank

July **August** **September** **October**
December **New Year's Eve**

1. In october it was cold.
2. Mr. Potts left on august 22 2018.
3. Every september they sell jam.
4. Ms. Down opened the shop on july 18 2018.
5. new year's eve is on december 31.

Proofreading Marks			
∧	Add	≡	Capital letter

Name ______________________________

Words with *oa*, *ow*

Read the word. Circle the picture that matches the word.

1. boat

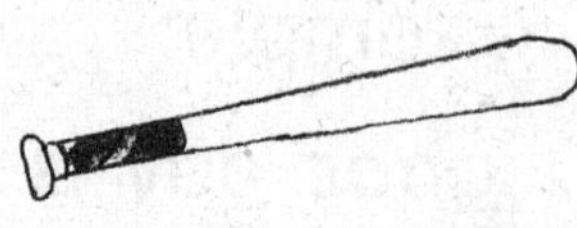

---

2. crow

---

3. goat

---

4. bowl

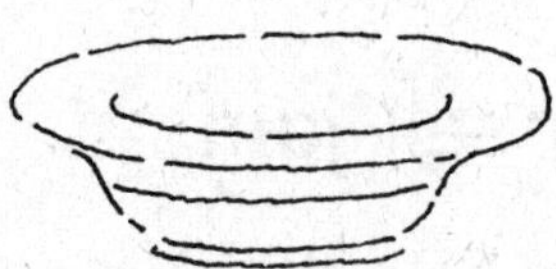

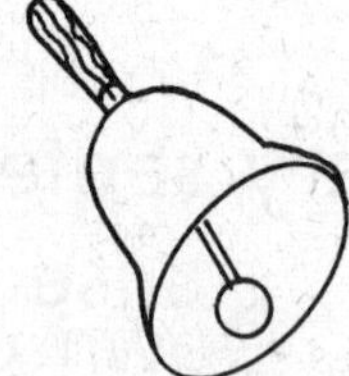

---

5. loaf

Name ____________________

Words to Know

Listen to the clues. Read along. Circle the best answer to each clue.

1. This means **finished.**	**paper**	**done**
2. This is in a short while.	**soon**	**great**
3. This means **speak.**	**were**	**talk**
4. **Awful** is its opposite.	**great**	**soon**
5. A joke makes you do this.	**laugh**	**done**
6. You write on this.	**work**	**paper**
7. This is a **job.**	**great**	**work**
8. Past tense for **are.**	**laugh**	**were**

Name ______________________

Tomás Rivera
Phonics: Words with *oa, ow*

Words with *oa*, *ow*

Circle the two words in each row that rhyme. Then write the letters that stand for the long o sound.

1. grow blow block gray ___ ___

2. slow sling throw thick ___ ___

3. much road load lunch ___ ___

4. coat got goat long ___ ___

5. flame show ground snow ___ ___

Name ______________________________

Spelling Words with Vowel Pairs *oa, ow*

Sort the words. Write the correct Spelling Words in each column.

Words with ow	Words with oa

Spelling Words

show
row
boat
blow
toad
road
low
coat
grow
snow

Name ______________________________

Future Using *will*

Circle the sentences that tell about the future. Rewrite the other sentences to tell about the future using *will*.

1. I read each day.

2. Brent will meet you at the shop.

3. My dad helps me read.

4. They washed the van.

5. Fran will beat the eggs.

____

6. ______________________________

____

7. ______________________________

____

8. ______________________________

____

Name ___________________________________

Order of Events

Draw pictures to show what you did to get ready for school today.

Write sentences about what you did to get ready for school today.

____

First, ___________________________________

____

Next, ___________________________________

____

Last, ___________________________________

Name ______________________

Contractions *'ve, 're*

Draw a line from each pair of words to its contraction.

You are	You're
They have	I've
I have	We're
We are	They've

Write a sentence using one of the contractions from above.

____

____

Name ____________________

Tomás Rivera
Phonics: Contractions *'ve, 're*

Contractions *'ve, 're*

Write the contraction that finishes each sentence.

1. ____________ all set for our big game.

   We are

2. ____________ my best friend.

   You are

3. ____________ had a lot of fun today!

   I have

4. ____________ had a lot of rain.

   They have

Tomás Rivera

Introducing Tomás Rivera

Let's make a sign for the Tomás Rivera Library!

Read pages 134–138. Tell people what was important to Tomás Rivera. Tell why the library has his name.

The Tomás Rivera Library

Name ______________________ Date ______

Read pages 139–141. Draw something that was important to Tomás Rivera. Write a caption for your drawing to tell why it was important.

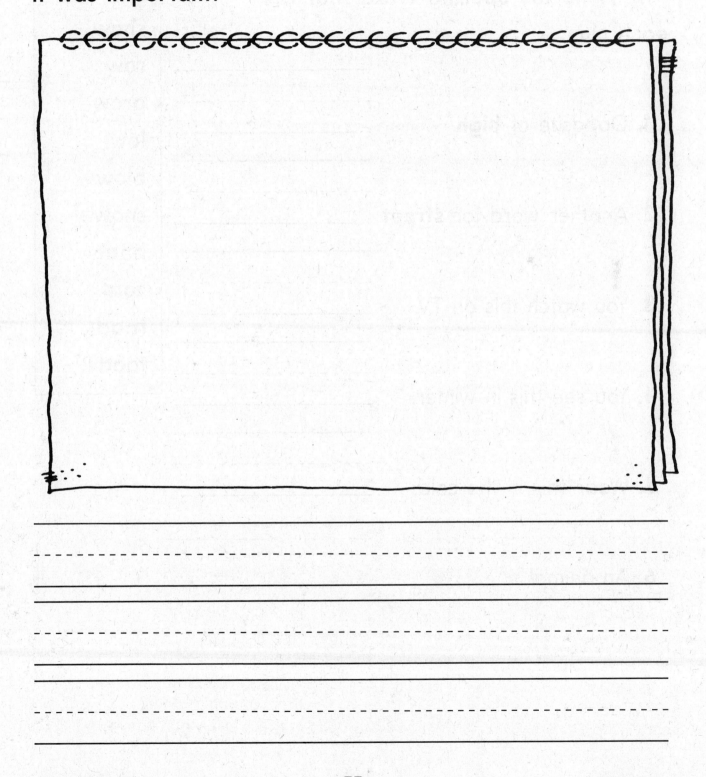

Name ______________________________

Spelling Words with Vowel Pairs *oa, ow*

Write the Spelling Word that fits each clue.

1. Opposite of **high** ______________

2. Another word for **street** ______________

3. You watch this on TV. ______________

4. You see this in winter. ______________

5. Wear this in the cold. ______________

6. An animal ______________

Spelling Words

show
row
grow
low
blow
snow
boat
coat
road
toad

Lesson 19
READER'S NOTEBOOK

Name ______________________

Tomás Rivera
Grammar: Verbs and Time

Future Using *going to*

Circle the sentences that tell about the future. Rewrite the other sentences to tell about the future. Use going to in each one.

1. I work with Ed.

2. Ed is going to have many crops.

3. My dad planted beets.

4. They pulled the weeds.

5. Jen is going to pick beans with Sam.

6. Tess has a pet cat.

____

7. ______________________

8. ______________________

9. ______________________

10. ______________________

Name ______________________________

Spelling Words with the Long *o* Sound

Write the correct word to complete each sentence.

1. The class will put on a ______________.

show **snow**

2. The ______________ hopped on the grass.

toad **load**

3. How do plants ______________?

throw **grow**

4. The ______________ came in with fish.

boat **bat**

5. Which ______________ will you sit in?

row **read**

Name ______________________

Spiral Review

Notice the clue word yesterday that tells about the past. Circle the verb that tells about the past. Then write those verbs.

1. **Yesterday** mom (works, worked) at the new shop.
2. She (opens, opened) the shop at nine.
3. Many kids (walk, walked) into the shop.
4. Val (asks, asked) for a new game.
5. Her mom (helps, helped) her.

Name

Tomás Rivera
Writing: Narrative Writing

Planning My Personal Narrative

Draw and write details that tell what happened first, next, and last.

My Topic: ______________________

First

Next

Last

Name ______________________

Grammar in Writing

You can write sentences that tell what may happen in the future. Use **will** or **is going to** to write sentences about the future.

Example: Jill walks.
Jill **will** walk.
Jill **is going to** walk.

Rewrite each sentence to tell about the future.

1. Tom runs far.

____

2. He went to work.

____

3. Grandpa sails his boat.

____

____

Name ____________________

Compound Words

Name each picture. Circle two words to make a compound for the picture. Write the compound word.

1. 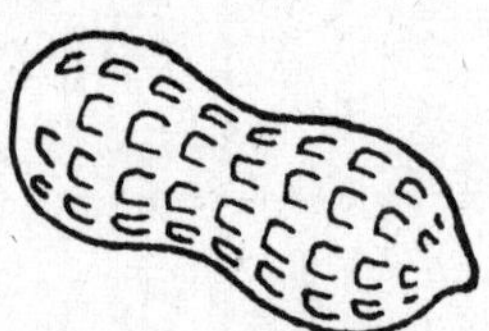

sea pea
nut side

2. 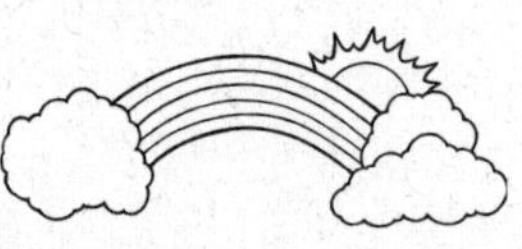

trail rain
bow mix

3. 

blue sea
bird shell

4. 

snow mail
box flake

5. 

cup sail
cake boat

Name ______________________________

Words to Know

Circle the best answer to each question.

1. What word goes with **less**?	**more**	**use**
2. What word goes with **dry**?	**door**	**wash**
3. What word goes with **open**?	**want**	**door**
4. What word goes with **father**?	**mother**	**more**
5. What word goes with **new**?	**old**	**wash**
6. What word goes with **need**?	**wash**	**want**
7. What word goes with **test**?	**more**	**try**
8. What word goes with **tools**?	**use**	**mother**

Name ______________________________

Compound Words

Choose words from the box to make a compound word to name each picture. Write the word. You will use some words more than once.

mail	rain	sail	sand	bow
row	boat	coat	box	

1. 

____

2. 

____

3. 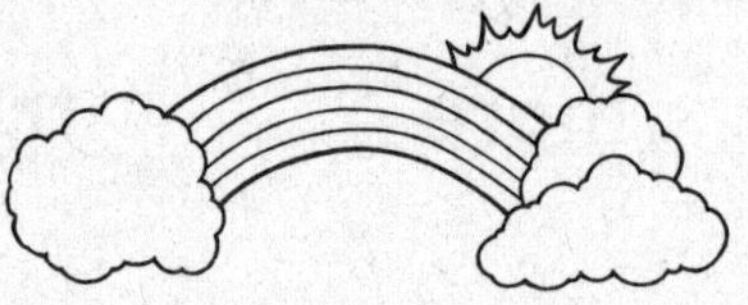

____

4. 

____

5. 

____

6. 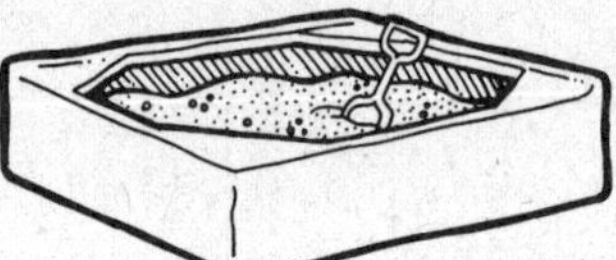

____

Name ____________________

Spelling Compound Words

Write the two words that make up each Spelling Word shown below.

1. bedtime ____________ ____________
2. himself ____________ ____________
3. flagpole ____________ ____________
4. sailboat ____________ ____________
5. backpack ____________ ____________
6. sunset ____________ ____________
7. raincoat ____________ ____________

Name ______________________________

Prepositional Phrases for Where

Circle the prepositional phase in each sentence. Write it on the line.

1. Rabbit went to Squirrel's home.

____

2. He went up the steps.

____

3. He knocked on the door.

____

Complete each sentence. Write a prepositional phrase that tells where.

4. The rabbit lives ______________________________.

5. The rabbit hopped ______________________________.

Name ______________________

Exact Details

Read each underlined detail. Write a more exact detail to finish each sentence.

1. I watched an animal.

   I watched ______________________.

2. I fed it some food.

   I fed it ______________________.

3. It moved around.

   It ______________________.

4. I will teach it something.

   I will teach it ______________________.

Name ________________________________

Words with Short Vowel /ĕ/*ea*

Little Rabbit's Tale
Phonics: Short *e* Sound Spelled *ea*

Circle two words that have the short e sound.

1. red bread bat rode

2. sled bone robe head

3. bed dead cube lot

4. peach fed Fred drink

5. led paint loaf thread

Name ______________________ Date ______

Little Rabbit's Tale

Goose and Beaver Tell the Tale

It is time for Goose and Beaver to tell the story!

Read pages 164–169. Tell this part of the story the way Goose would tell it. Tell how Goose feels and what happens.

Name ______________________ Date ______

Read pages 174–179. Tell the end of the story like Beaver would tell it. Why is Beaver unhappy at Little Rabbit's house? What happens next?

Name ________________________________

Spelling Compound Words

Draw a line from a word on the left to a word on the right to make each Spelling Word.

1. bath	time
2. flag	tub
3. bed	pole
4. sun	pack
5. back	set
6. play	coat
7. rain	pen
8. sail	side
9. in	self
10. him	boat

Spelling Words

- bedtime
- sunset
- bathtub
- sailboat
- flagpole
- backpack
- playpen
- raincoat
- inside
- himself

Name ____________________

Prepositional Phrases

Circle the prepositional phrase in each sentence. Decide if the prepositional phrase tells where or when. Write where or when on the line.

1. The friends play after lunch. ____________

2. They meet at Viv's home. ____________

3. Viv swings under a tree. ____________

4. Lin skips on the grass. ____________

5. Mom comes home at five o'clock. ____________

6. Lin goes home before then. ____________

Name ______________________________

Spelling Compound Words

Write the correct word to complete each sentence.

1. The ______________ was very red.

   sunset **himself**

2. Let us play ______________ today.

   inside **flagpole**

3. I carry my ______________ with me.

   playpen **backpack**

4. Before ______________ I brush my teeth.

   bedtime **sailboat**

5. My ______________ has a matching hat.

   bathtub **raincoat**

Name ______________________________

Spiral Review

Write each sentence with the correct verb.

1. This puppet (is, are) small.

2. Raindrops (is, are) wet.

3. The lambs (is, are) white.

4. The show (was, were) funny.

5. Those muffins (was, were) huge.

Name ______________________

Grammar in Writing

A prepositional phrase can tell when or where.

Example: We walk **after lunch**. when

We walk **in the park**. where

Add a prepositional phrase to each sentence to tell when or where. Write the new sentence on the line.

1. My friends and I ran.

____

2. Something fell.

____

3. I tripped.

____

4. I went home.

____

Name ______________________________ Date ______

Amazing Whales!

What I Know About Whales

Draw your favorite whale. Label your picture. Tell one fact that makes this whale amazing.

Kind of whale

____

____

Amazing Fact

____

____

Name ______________________ Date ______

Whales are in trouble! Write three things people can do to help them.

1. ______________________________

2. ______________________________

3. ______________________________

Name ______________________________________

Words with *ar*

Circle the word that matches the picture.

1.

cat card

2.

star stamp

3.

march much

4.

barn bark

5.

arm art

6.

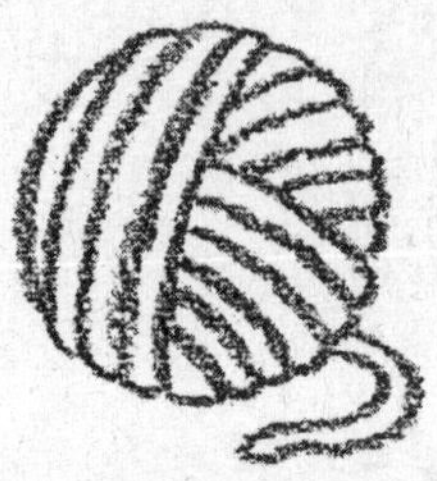

yard yarn

Name ______________________________

Words to Know

Circle the correct word to complete each sentence.

1. Dad reads us a funny (story, noise).

2. The children are making a lot of (loudly, noise).

3. Tim's parents are planning a trip around the (world, window).

4. Those children are talking (loudly, story) in class.

5. I (few, shall) be late for school tomorrow.

6. Some animals hunt at (night, world).

7. Close your (night, window) when it rains.

8. (Few, Shall) birds can swim.

Name ______________________________

Words with *ar*

 **Look at the picture and read the words.**

Write the word that matches the picture.

1.

stem   start

____

2.

cat   cart

____

3.

car   card

____

4.

shake   shark

____

5.

pack   park

____

Name ______________________

Spelling Words with *r*-Controlled Vowel *ar*

Spelling Words

far
arm
yard
art
jar
bar
barn
bark
card
yarn

Write the Spelling Words that rhyme with **far**, **yard**, and **barn**.

1. **Far** rhymes with ______________________

and ______________________ .

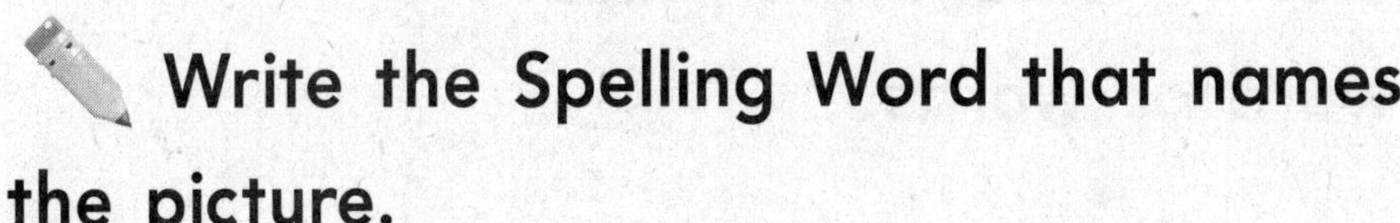

2. **Yard** rhymes with ______________________ .

3. **Barn** rhymes with ______________________ .

Write the Spelling Word that names the picture.

4. 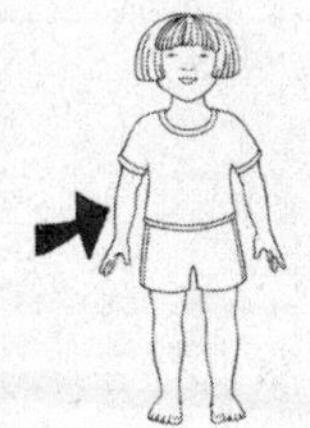
____

5. 
____

6. 
____

Name ____________________

Pronouns That Name One

Circle the pronoun that can take the place of the underlined word or words.

1. Grandpa makes a shed.

   He **She** **It**

2. The shed is short and wide.

   He **She** **It**

3. Ann helps Grandpa work in the shed.

   He **She** **It**

Write He, She, or It to take the place of the underlined word or words.

4. Joe sees a nest.

   ____________ sees a nest.

5. The nest has eggs.

   ____________ has eggs.

Name ______________________________

Dialogue

Think of another problem that Toad could have with his garden. Then write what he and Frog might have said.

Toad still needed help with his garden. He asked Frog what to do. "______________________________

______________________________ ?" Toad asked.

"______________________________

______________________________ ," said Frog.

Name ___________________________________

Words with *or*, *ore*

Read the sentences. Circle the sentence that tells about the picture.

1. We look at the score.

We look at the star.

2. I like to do chores.

I snore when I sleep.

3. She finds shells at the shore.

She finds fish at the shop.

4. He can play the thorn.

He can play the horn.

5. Here is a jar.

Here is a fork.

Name ______________________ Date ______

The Garden

Could That Really Happen?

Think about the story and what could happen in real life.

Read pages 15–18. Read what happens. Decide if it could happen in real life. Tell why or why not.

What Happens	Could this happen in real life? Why or why not?
A frog and toad talk to each other.	
The seeds did not grow right after they were put in the ground.	

Name ______________________ Date ______

Read pages 19–29. Fill in the chart.

What Happens	Could this happen in real life? Why or why not?
Frog said that shouting at the seeds kept them from growing.	
The seeds were afraid of the dark.	
Letting the sun shine on the seeds and the rain fall on them helped them grow.	

Name ______________________________

Spelling Words with *r*-Controlled Vowel *ar*

Spelling Words

- far
- arm
- yard
- art
- jar
- bar
- barn
- bark
- card
- yarn

Write the Spelling Word that names the picture.

1.

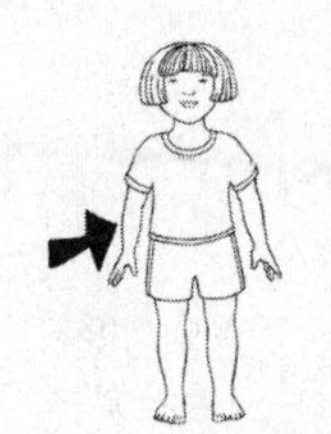

____

2.

____

3.

____

4.

____

5.

____

6.

____

Name ___

Pronouns That Name More Than One

Circle the pronoun that can take the place of each underlined subject.

1. Workers plant trees in the park.

   We **They**

2. The trees grow big.

   We **They**

3. Sis and I sit under the trees.

   We **They**

Write We or They to take the place of each underlined subject.

4. Dad and I walk to the park.

   ___ walk to the park.

5. Pete and Kate run and play.

   ___ run and play.

Name ____________________

Planning My Sentences

Write and draw details that tell what happened first and next.

Topic: After Toad's garden started to grow,

____

Frog and Toad ____________________.

First

Next

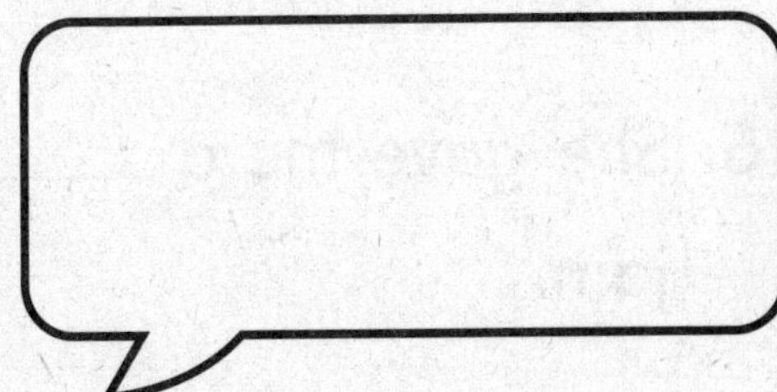

Name ______________________

Lesson 21
READER'S NOTEBOOK

The Garden
Spelling: Words with *ar*

Spelling Words with *r*-Controlled Vowel *ar*

Write the correct word to complete each sentence.

1. She lives ______________ away from me. (fun, far)
2. He waves his ______________ in the air. (ants, arm)
3. We play in the ______________. (yard, yarn)
4. We paint in ______________ class. (art, part)
5. She gave me a ______________ of jam. (bar, jar)
6. Hang your coats on the ______________. (card, bar)
7. The sheep are in the ______________. (barn, big)

Name ______________________________

Spiral Review

Draw a line under each question.

1. What sort of tree is this?
2. Do all trees have leaves?
3. Pine trees have cones.
4. What animals live in trees?
5. Birds live in trees.
6. Do we need trees?
7. Trees give us air.
8. Do we get food from trees?

Name ______________________________

Grammar in Writing

The Garden
Grammar: Subject Pronouns

The pronouns **he, she,** and **it** name one. The pronouns **we** and **they** name more than one.

Fix the mistakes in the sentences. Use proofreading marks.

Example: The shed is done. ~~She~~ ^It looks nice.

1. Mom saws. He makes a shelf for the shed.

2. Bob and I get paint. They paint the shelf.

3. Mom has some grapes. It puts them in a bowl.

4. My friends come over. We want to see the shed.

Proofreading Marks	
^	add
(strike-through mark)	take out

Name ____________________

Amazing Animals
Phonics: *r*-Controlled Vowels *er, ir, ur*

Words with *er*, *ir*, *ur*

Read the word. Circle the picture that matches the word.

1. bird	
2. turn	
3. her	
4. burn	
5. third	
6. herd	

Name ______________________________

Words to Know

Circle the word that best completes each sentence.

1. I like (until, learning) about animals.

2. Our dog Pip is five (follow, years) old.

3. Pip has (baby, eight) new pups.

4. She will feed her pups (until, learning) they are older.

5. A (eight, young) kitten came to our home.

6. The new kitten likes to (until, follow) Pip.

7. The kitten (begins, learning) to think he is Pip's pup!

8. The new kitten is not Pip's (years, baby).

Name ______________________

Amazing Animals
Phonics: *r*-Controlled Vowels *er, ir, ur*

Words with *er*, *ir*, *ur*

Read the words in the box. Write the word that matches the picture.

clerk	shirt	stir	hurt	curl

1. ______________________

2. ______________________

3. ______________________

4. ______________________

5.  ______________________

Name ______________________

Spelling Words with *r*-Controlled Vowels *er*, *ir*, *ur*

Spelling Words

- sir
- fern
- girl
- her
- third
- hurt
- fur
- bird
- turn
- stir

Write the Spelling Words with er.

1. ______________ 2. ______________

Write the Spelling Words with ir.

3. ______________ 4. ______________

5. ______________ 6. ______________

7. ______________

Write the Spelling Words with ur.

8. ______________ 9. ______________

10. ______________

Name ____________________

Amazing Animals
Grammar: The Pronouns *I* and *Me*

Naming Yourself Last

Circle the correct words to finish each sentence.

1. ______ see the goat.

Jean and me **Jean and I**

2. Dad took ______ to the zoo.

I and Steve **Steve and me**

3. ______ look at the ducks.

Rex and I **Rex and me**

Write the words from the word box to finish the sentence.

Ann	I

4. ____________________ and ____________________

hold the baby snakes.

Name ______________________________

Exact Verbs

Amazing Animals
Writing: Narrative Writing

Draw a picture of an animal for a story. Give your animal a name.

Name: ______________________________

Finish these story sentences about your animal. Use exact verbs.

______________ is a ______________.
name — kind of animal

______________ likes to ______________.
name — exact verb

______________ always ______________ a lot!
name — exact verb

Name ____________________

Amazing Animals
Phonics: *r*-Controlled Vowels *er, ir, ur*

Words with *er*, *ir*, *ur*

Choose a word from the box to name each picture. Write the word.

girl	turn	chirp	third	hers	dirt

1. ____________________

2. ____________________

3. ____________________

4. ____________________

5. ____________________

6. ____________________

Name ______________________ Date ______

Amazing Animals

Where Is My Home?

The animals got mixed up! Write where each animal lives. Then, write the clues you used to figure out the answer.

pond	ocean	arctic	desert	grassland

Read pages 48–50.
Where is the bear's home? ______________
What clues did you use?

____

____

Read pages 51–54. Where is the camel's home? ______________
What clues did you use?

____

____

Name ______________________ Date ______

Amazing Animals
Independent Reading

Read pages 55–56.
Where is the duck's home?
What clues did you use?

Read pages 57–58.
Where is the giraffe's home?
What clues did you use?

Read pages 59–65.
Where is the dolphin's home? What clues did you use?

Name ______________________________

Amazing Animals
Spelling: Words with *er, ir, ur*

Spelling Words with *r*-Controlled Vowels *er*, *ir*, *ur*

Spelling Words

her
fern
girl
sir
stir
bird
fur
hurt
turn
third

Write the Spelling Word that fits each clue.

1. Opposite of **boy** ______________

2. Goes with **pain** ______________

3. What a bear has ______________

4. Goes with **three** ______________

5. Opposite of **him** ______________

6. An animal ______________

Name ___________________________

Amazing Animals
Grammar: The Pronouns *I* and *Me*

Naming Yourself with *I*

Write the sentences correctly.

1. Jay and me visit a farm.

____

2. Me and Bree feed the ducks.

____

3. Dave and me pet the sheep.

____

4. Me and Ed see the lambs.

____

5. Meg and me hold the cat.

____

Name ____________________

Planning My Sentences

Write and draw details that tell what happened first and next.

My Topic: I will write about a

____.

First

Next

This is how my story will end:

Name ______________________________

Spelling Words with *r*-Controlled Vowels *er*, *ir*, *ur*

Spelling Words

- her
- fern
- stir
- fur
- hurt
- turn
- third
- girl
- sir
- bird

Write the Spelling Word that completes each sentence.

1. I like ______________ dress.
2. I watered the ______________ .
3. The ______________ has a pink doll.
4. I fell and ______________ my arm.
5. The ______________ laid three eggs.
6. The cat has thick ______________ .

Name ______________________________

Spiral Review

Draw a line under the two shorter sentences in each compound sentence.

1. Can we go to the zoo, or is it too cold?
2. I want to see the ducks, but they want to see the foxes.
3. Sit quietly, and eat your snack.

Write a compound sentence by combining the two shorter sentences.

4. Dad baked a cake. We helped him.

______________________________ and

____

Name ______________________________

Amazing Animals
Grammar: The Pronouns *I* and *Me*

Grammar in Writing

Use the pronoun **I** in the subject of a sentence. Use the pronoun **me** in the predicate of a sentence. Name yourself last.

Fix the mistakes in these sentences. Use proofreading marks.

Example: ~~Me~~ (Ted) and ~~Ted~~ (I) see the ducklings.

1. I and Mark feed the pups.

2. Mom helps me and Jon at the zoo.

3. Me and Hing look at the piglets.

4. Kris and i see the baby birds.

Proofreading Marks	
∧	add
℘	take out
≡	capital letter

Name ______________________________________

Whistle for Willie
Phonics: Vowel Digraph /o͝o/*oo*

The Vowel Sound *oo* *(book)*

Circle the word that matches the picture.

1.

book hook

2.

book cook

3.

wool wood

4.

hook hood

5.

brook took

6.

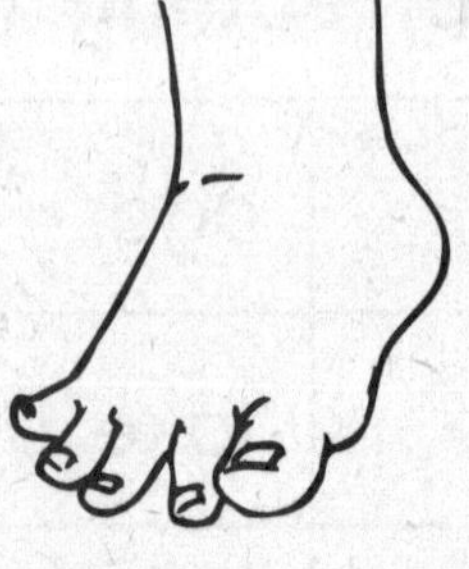

soot foot

Name ______________________________

Words to Know

Circle the word that best completes each sentence.

1. We can go to the play (together, boy).

2. The box has (began, nothing) in it.

3. The new (boy, along) is named Dan.

4. Dan and his (together, father) like to fish.

5. My (house, nothing) has a blue door.

6. Jan skipped (house, along) the path.

7. I will sing the song (again, boy).

8. A bell (house, began) to ring.

Name ________________________________

Words with *oo (book)*

Whistle for Willie
Phonics: Vowel Digraph /o͝o/*oo*

Circle the sentence that matches the picture.

1. We cook at mealtime.

We look at the time.

2. I see a little brook.

I see a little book.

3. He has a hat made of wool.

He has a box made of wood.

4. Put your coat on a hook.

Put your coat in a hood.

5. Wash off that soot.

Wash off your foot.

Name ______________________________

Spelling Words with Vowel Digraph *oo*

Sort the words. Write the correct Spelling Words in each column.

Words with **ook**	Words with **ood**

Spelling Words

look
book
good
hook
brook
took
foot
shook
wood
hood

Name ____________________

Whistle for Willie
Grammar: Possessive Pronouns

Using *my*, *your*, *his*, and *her*

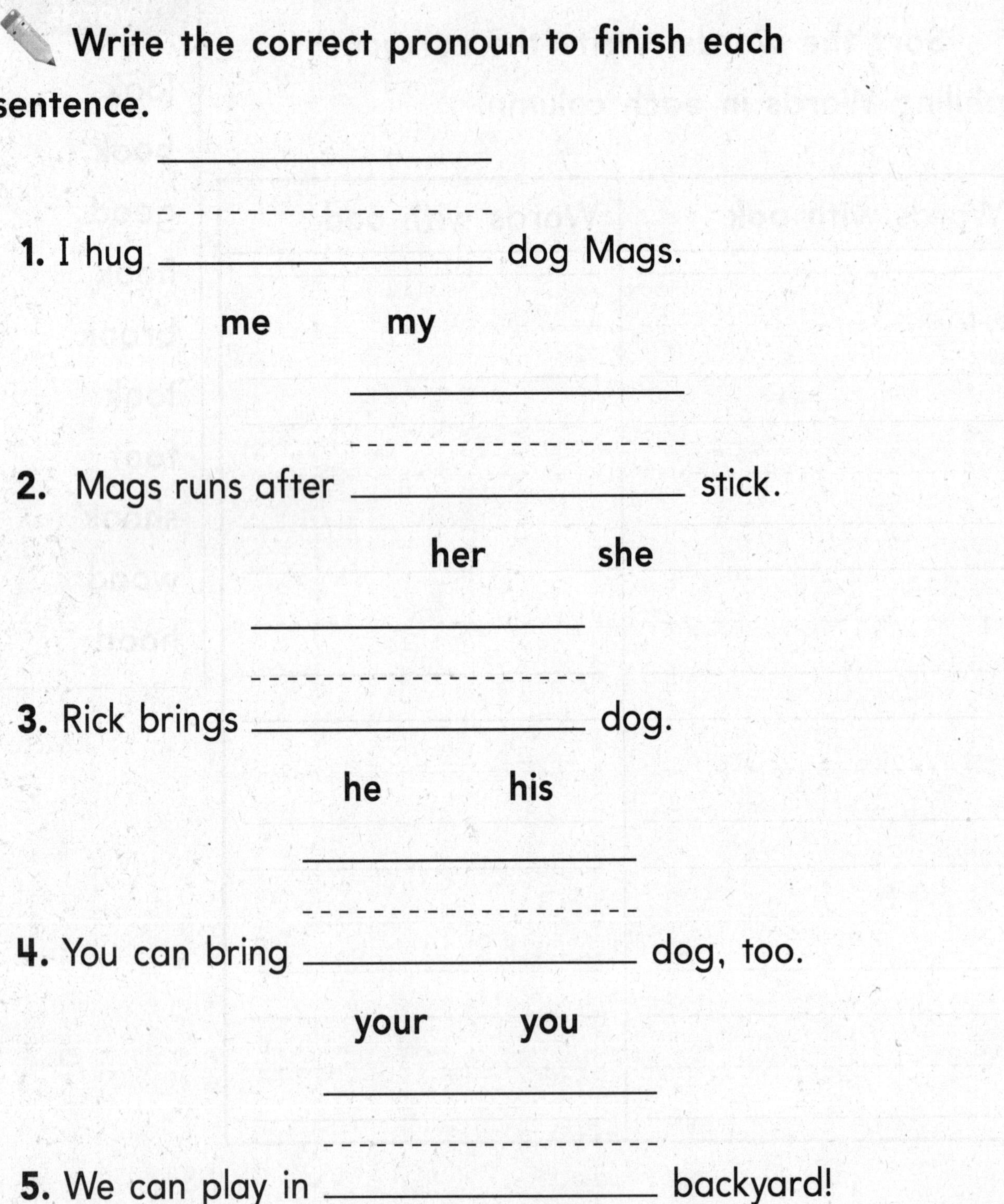

Write the correct pronoun to finish each sentence.

1. I hug ____________ dog Mags.

me **my**

2. Mags runs after ____________ stick.

her **she**

3. Rick brings ____________ dog.

he **his**

4. You can bring ____________ dog, too.

your **you**

5. We can play in ____________ backyard!

they **my**

Name ______________________________

Whistle for Willie
Writing: Narrative Writing

Order of Events

Finish the sentences. Give a summary of the first part of Whistle for Willie.

Peter wished ______________________________.

He tried ______________________________.

When Peter saw Willie, he ______________________________.

Then, Willie ______________________________.

Name ____________________

Whistle for Willie
Phonics: Syllable Pattern CVC

How Many Syllables?

Read each word. Circle how many syllables it has. Hint: Each time you hear a vowel sound, there is a syllable.

1. hammer 1 2	**2.** doctor 1 2
3. stood 1 2	**4.** rabbit 1 2
5. mister 1 2	**6.** third 1 2

Name ______________________ Date ______

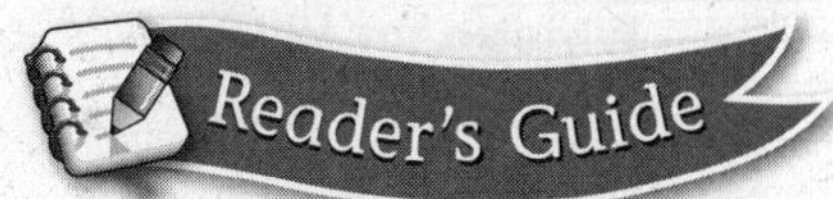

Whistle for Willie

Picture Words

Good readers make pictures in their mind as they read.

Read pages 83–87. Draw what Peter is doing on page 86. Write the words that help you picture it.

Name ______________________ Date ______

Read pages 88–91. Do you see the cat? Write how the cat might describe what it sees and hears Peter doing.

Read pages 92–103. Then look back at pages 96–97. Write how Willie might describe what he sees and hears.

Name ______________________________

Spelling Words with Vowel Digraph *oo*

Write each group of Spelling Words in ABC order.

look hood good wood book	shook hook foot brook took

Spelling Words

look
book
good
hook
brook
took
foot
shook
wood
hood

Name ______________________________

Using *mine*, *yours*, *his*, *hers*, and *theirs*

Write the correct pronoun to finish each sentence.

1. This mitt is ______________.

   your **yours**

2. The bat is ______________.

   he **his**

3. That treat is ______________.

   their **theirs**

4. This house is ______________.

   my **mine**

5. That dog is ______________.

   hers **her**

Name ______________________

Planning My Summary

Write sentences and draw details for your summary of Whistle for Willie.

My Topic: ______________________

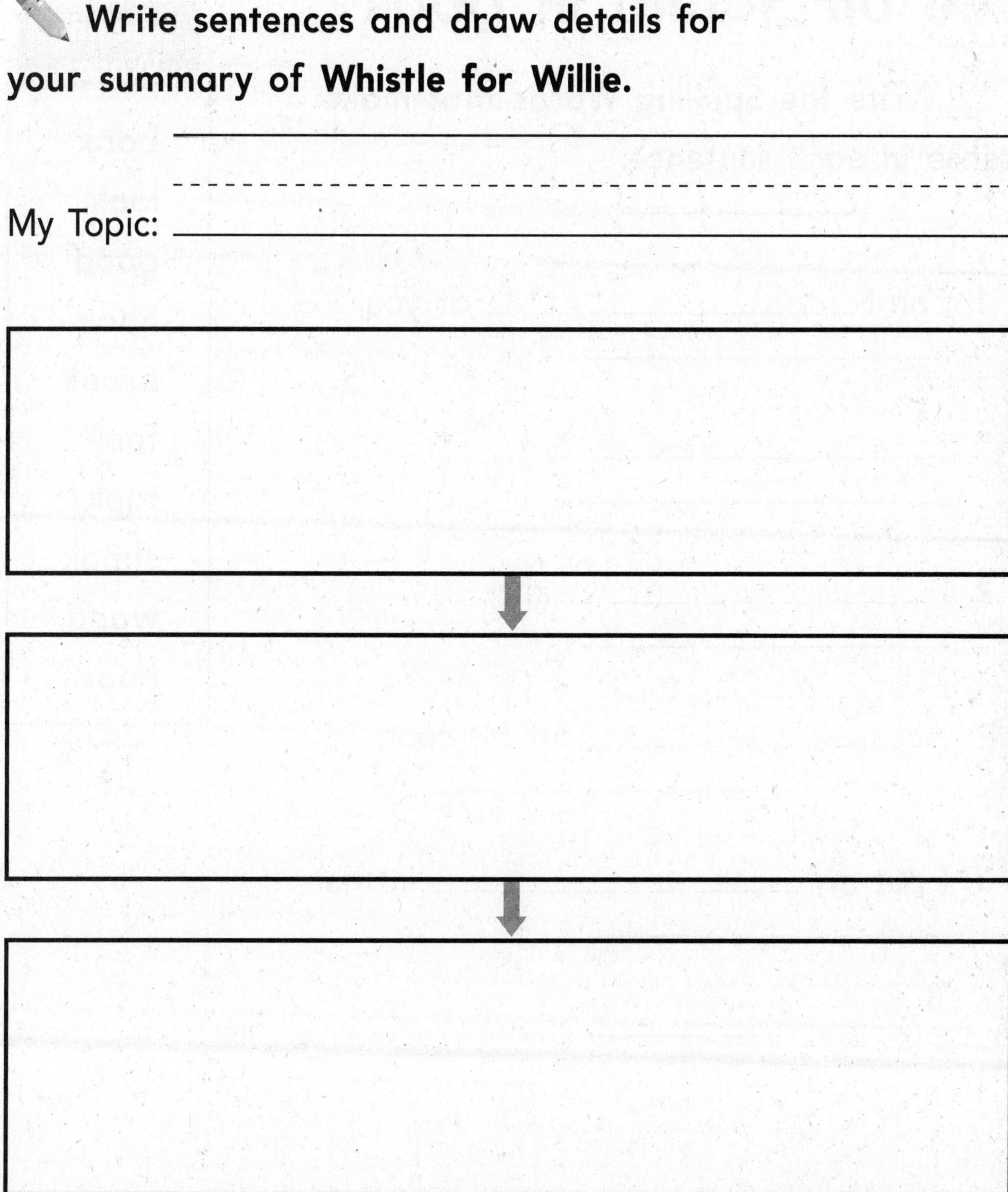

Name ______________________________

Spelling Words with the *oo* Sound in *book*

Write the Spelling Words that make sense in each sentence.

1. Can I ____________ at your ____________?

2. I ____________ the ____________ off his coat.

3. I put my ____________ in the ____________.

Spelling Words

- book
- look
- good
- hook
- brook
- foot
- took
- shook
- wood
- hood

Name ____________________

Spiral Review

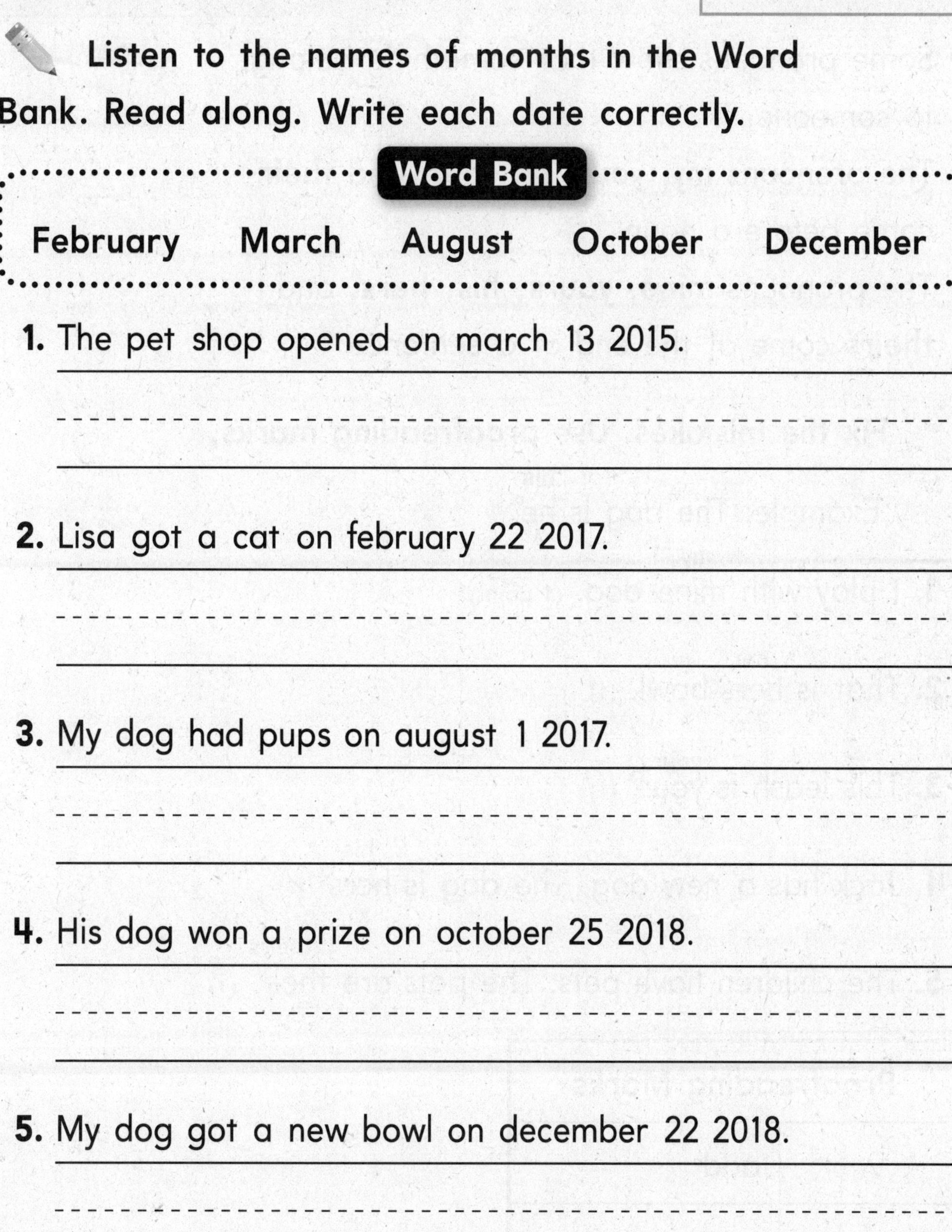

Listen to the names of months in the Word Bank. Read along. Write each date correctly.

Word Bank

February March August October December

1. The pet shop opened on march 13 2015.

2. Lisa got a cat on february 22 2017.

3. My dog had pups on august 1 2017.

4. His dog won a prize on october 25 2018.

5. My dog got a new bowl on december 22 2018.

Name ____________________

Grammar in Writing

- Some pronouns show that something belongs to someone.
- The pronouns **my, your, his, her,** and **their** come before a noun.
- The pronouns **mine, yours, his, hers,** and **theirs** come at the end of a sentence.

Fix the mistakes. Use proofreading marks.

Example: The dog is ~~he~~ **his**.

1. I play with ~~mine~~ **my** dog. **(1 point)**
2. That is ~~hers~~ **her** bowl. **(1)**
3. This leash is ~~your~~ **yours**. **(1)**
4. Jack has a new dog. The dog is ~~hers~~ **his**. **(1)**
5. The children have pets. The pets are ~~their~~ **theirs**. **(1)**

Proofreading Marks	
∧	add
—ↄ	take out

Read directions to children.

Assessment Tip: Total 5 points

Name ____________________

Words with *oo (moon)*, *ou*, *ew*

Circle the word that names the picture.

1.

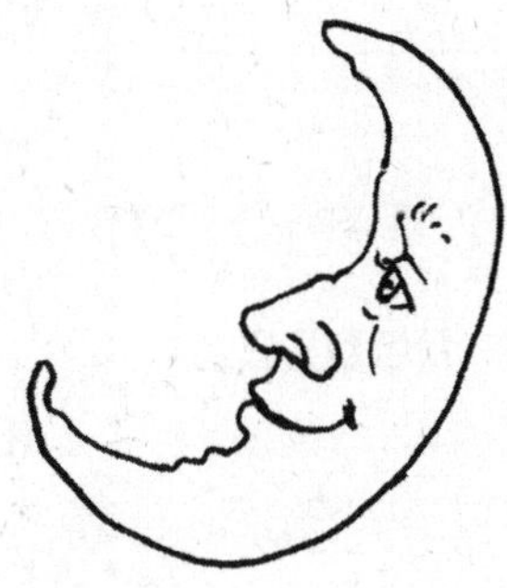

moth moon

2.

spoon spot

3.

scream screw

4.

soap soup

5.

boat boot

6.

stool stole

Name ______________________

Words to Know

Write a word from the box to complete each sentence.

Words to Know

almost
country
covered
earth
kinds
ready
soil
warms

1. I planted flowers in the ______________.

2. Our heater ______________ our house.

3. Pete ______________ hit a home run.

4. Mr. Lee lives in the ______________.

5. Mom ______________ us with a blanket.

6. Are you ______________ to go?

7. Dinosaurs walked the ______________ millions of years ago.

8. I got many ______________ of games for my birthday.

Name ______________________________

Words with *oo (moon)*, *ou*, *ew*

Write the word that best completes each sentence. Use the words in the Word Bank.

Word Bank

cool   group   room   drew   stool

1. I got together with a ______________ of friends.
2. We had fun playing in my ______________.
3. We ______________ some pictures and hung them up.
4. Then we painted my old ______________.
5. Now the room looks ______________!

Name ______________________________

Spelling Words with Vowel Digraphs *oo, ou, ew*

Spelling Words

- soon
- new
- noon
- zoo
- boot
- too
- moon
- blew
- soup
- you

Write the Spelling Words with ou.

1. ______________ 2. ______________

Write the Spelling Words with ew.

3. ______________ 4. ______________

Write the Spelling Words with oo.

5. ______________ 6. ______________

7. ______________ 8. ______________

9. ______________ 10. ______________

Name ______________________________

Indefinite Pronouns

Indefinite pronouns are special pronouns that stand for people or things that are not named.

Word Bank

anyone	**someone**	**everything**
something	**everybody**	**somebody**

Draw a line under the indefinite pronoun in each sentence.

1. He knows everything about trees.
2. Would anyone like an apple?
3. Someone baked apple pie.

Write an indefinite pronoun from the Word Bank to complete each sentence.

4. I learned ______________ about trees.
5. Has ______________ picked apples before?

Name ______________________________

Describing Characters

Write clear details to finish the story. Some details should describe Rex and Grace.

Rex was a ______________ dog. He lived with

a ______________ girl named Grace. Grace

liked to sit under the ______________ apple

tree in her yard. Grace wanted to teach Rex

to ______________ with her. She told Rex

to ______________ . When Rex did the trick,

Grace told Rex, "______________ !" Rex wagged

his ______________ tail.

Name ____________________

Words with *ue*, *u*, *u_e*

Circle the two words in each row that have the same vowel sound.
Write the letters that stand for the sound.

				ue u u-e
1.	clue	trust	true	____ ____
2.	prune	flute	float	____ ____
3.	goal	flu	truth	____ ____
4.	tone	tune	rule	____ ____
5.	blue	blunt	glue	____ ____

Name ______________________ Date ______

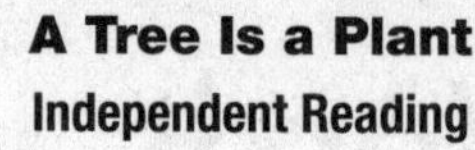

A Tree Is a Plant
Independent Reading

A Tree Is a Plant

Tree Diagrams

Read pages 136–137. Draw a tree with leaves and roots. Use green arrows to show how food moves. Use blue arrows to show how water moves.

Name ______________________ Date ______

Read pages 128–147. Draw the apple tree in each season. Start with spring. Write the name of each season.

Name ______________________________

Spelling Words with Vowel Digraphs *oo*, *ou*, *ew*

Write each group of Spelling Words in ABC order.

soon moon noon zoo boot	too new blew soup you
______	______
______	______
______	______
______	______
______	______

Spelling Words

- soon
- new
- noon
- zoo
- boot
- too
- moon
- blew
- soup
- you

Name ______________________

Indefinite Pronouns

A Tree Is a Plant
Grammar: Indefinite Pronouns

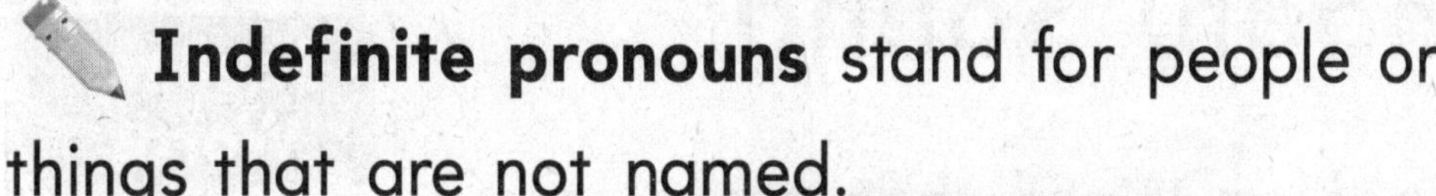

Indefinite pronouns stand for people or things that are not named.

Word Bank

anyone	**someone**	**everyone**
something	**everybody**	**everything**

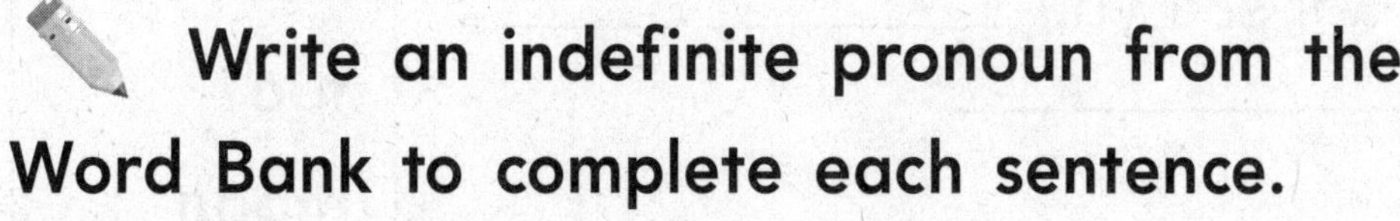

Write an indefinite pronoun from the Word Bank to complete each sentence.

1. We met ______________ in the park.

2. Did you bring ______________ to eat.

3. Can ______________ pick apples with me?

4. I put ______________ in the box.

5. ______________ likes red apples.

Name ____________________

Spelling Words with the *oo* (moon) Sound

Spelling Words

- soon
- new
- noon
- zoo
- boot
- too
- moon
- blew
- soup
- you

Write the Spelling Word that completes each sentence.

1. We will have our lunch at ____________ .
2. I hope that I will see you ____________ .
3. The wind ____________ the tree over.
4. I saw many animals at the ____________ .
5. There was a full ____________ last night.
6. It is ____________ hot to play outside.
7. We will have ____________ for lunch.
8. I need a ____________ pencil.

Name ______

Spiral Review

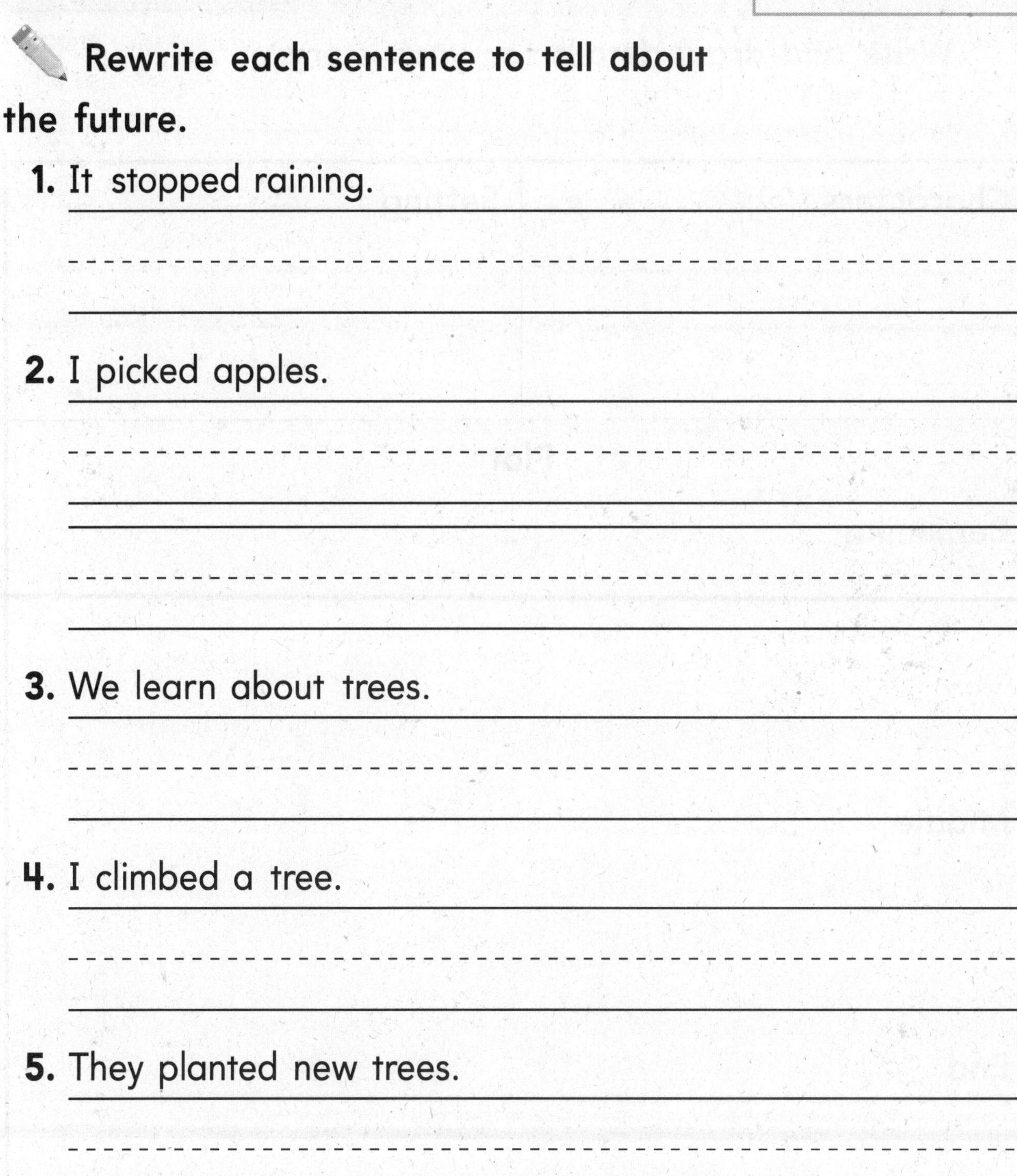

Rewrite each sentence to tell about the future.

1. It stopped raining.

2. I picked apples.

3. We learn about trees.

4. I climbed a tree.

5. They planted new trees.

Name ______________________________

Planning My Story

Write and draw details for your story.

Characters	Setting

Plot

Beginning

Middle

End

Name ______________________________

Grammar in Writing

Use **indefinite pronouns** to stand for the names of people or things. They do not name certain people or things.

Word Bank

anyone	**something**	**someone**
everything	**everyone**	**everybody**

Write an indefinite pronoun from the Word Bank to complete each sentence.

1. ______________ went to the farm.

2. The farmer knew ______________ about apples.

3. She helped ______________ pick apples.

4. She didn't want ______________ to get hurt.

Name ____________________________________

Words with *ou*, *ow*

Circle the word that names the picture.

1.

cot cow

2.

couch coach

3.

moose mouse

4.

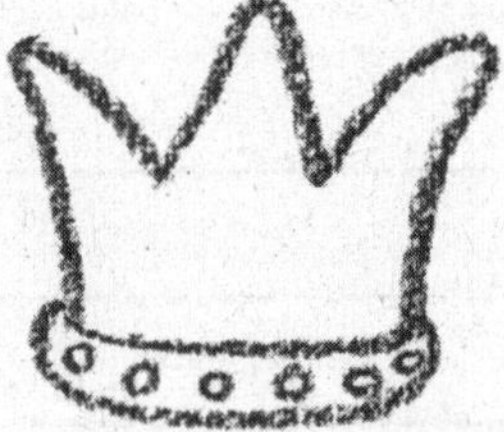

crow crown

5.

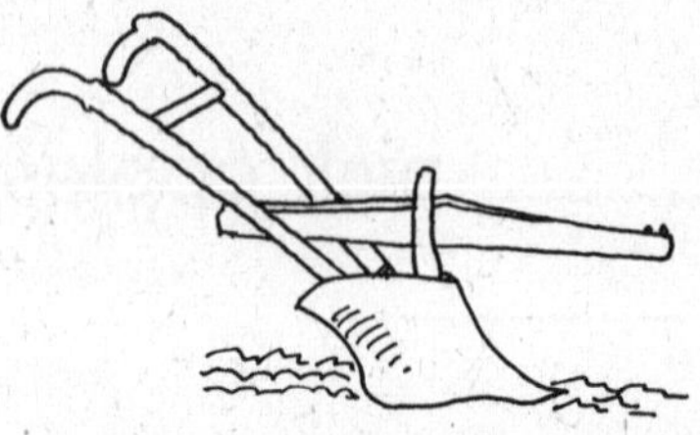

plate plow

6.

cloud closed

Name ____________________

Words to Know

The New Friend
High-Frequency Words

Draw a line to match each picture to the word that goes with it.

1.  family

2.  school

3. 

party

4.  city

5. 

buy

6. myself

Use the words **seven** and **please** together in a sentence. Write it on the line.

____

____

Name ____________________

Words with *ou, ow*

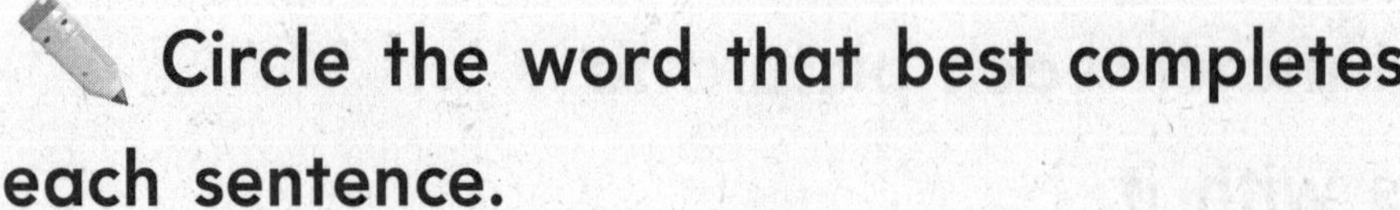

Circle the word that best completes each sentence.

1. I got a new pet. He's a _____ dog.

hound **hold**

2. He should not jump up on the _____.

coach **couch**

3. At night, my dog _____ at the moon.

holes **howls**

4. My dog's bark is very _____.

loud **load**

5. He will _____ when someone comes to the house!

grow **growl**

6. He sits when I tell him to get _____.

down **dome**

Name ______________________________

Spelling Words with Vowel Diphthongs *ow*, *ou*

Sort the words. Write the correct Spelling Words in each column.

Words with ou	Words with ow

Spelling Words

how
now
cow
owl
ouch
house
found
out
gown
town

Name ____________________

Contractions with *not*

Write a contraction from the box for the underlined word or words.

Word Bank

isn't
aren't
can't
don't

1. This house is not empty now.

____

2. I do not know where my books are.

____

3. They are not in this big box.

____

4. I cannot find my jump rope.

____

5. I do not have a new friend yet.

____

Name ___

The New Friend
Writing: Narrative Writing

Sentences with Different Lengths

Make long sentences by joining two short sentences with and.

1. Kirk moved to a new city. He was happy.

___,
and ___.

2. The city is far away. It is very big.

___,
and ___.

3. Kirk made new friends. He saw new places.

___,
and ___.

Name ______________________________

Words with *oi*, *oy*, *au*, *aw*

Circle the two words in each row that have the same vowel sound. Write the letters that stand for the sound.

		oi oy au aw
1.	coins coats join	____ ____
2.	joy boy book	____ ____
3.	house sauce pause	____ ____
4.	dune dawn crawl	____ ____
5.	point paint moist	____ ____

Name ______________________ Date ______

The New Friend

Meet Makoto!

You get to introduce Makoto to his classmates!

Read pages 166–173. Write three things you know about Makoto. Draw a picture of him.

Name ______________________________ Date ______

Read pages 174–181. Makoto wants to bring something to show the class more about his life. Draw a picture to show what he brings. Then write a sentence to tell why he chose it.

Name ______________________

Spelling Words with Vowel Diphthongs *ou, ow*

Write the Spelling Word that fits each clue.

Spelling Words

- how
- now
- cow
- owl
- ouch
- house
- found
- out
- gown
- town

1. Opposite of **later** ______________________

2. Opposite of **lost** ______________________

3. A farm animal ______________________

4. Smaller than a city ______________________

5. Opposite of **in** ______________________

6. A bird ______________________

Name ______________________

Contractions with Pronouns

 **Write a contraction from the box for the underlined words.**

Word Bank

I'm	he's	she's	it's

1. It is a pretty day.

   ____

2. I am going to school with my new friend.

   ____

3. He is in the car with his mom.

   ____

4. She is driving us.

   ____

Name ______________________

Spelling Words with *ow* and *ou*

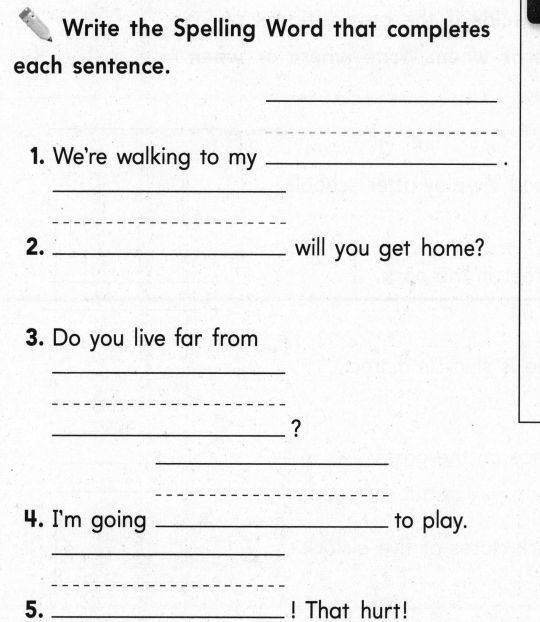

Write the Spelling Word that completes each sentence.

1. We're walking to my ______________.
2. ______________ will you get home?
3. Do you live far from ______________?
4. I'm going ______________ to play.
5. ______________! That hurt!
6. He's coming home right ______________.

Spelling Words

- how
- house
- now
- owl
- cow
- found
- town
- ouch
- out
- gown

Name ______________________________

Spiral Review

Circle the prepositional phrase in each sentence. Decide if the prepositional phrase tells where or when. Write where or when on the line.

1. Max and Viv play after school. ______________

2. They meet in the park. ______________

3. Viv's kite is stuck in a tree. ______________

4. They race on the grass. ______________

5. The park closes at five o'clock. ______________

6. The friends will meet again next week. ______________

Name ______________________________

Grammar in Writing

- A contraction is a short way of writing some words.
- This mark (') takes the place of missing letters.

Fix the mistakes in these sentences. Use proofreading marks.

Example: ~~H'es~~ He's in a new house.

1. Im' with my new friend.
2. Today shes putting her toys away.
3. She cant' find the games.
4. The books are'nt in the box.
5. We do'nt play today.

Proofreading Marks	
∧	add
⌒	take out

Name ______________________________

Adding *-ed*, *-ing*

Look at the picture. Read the word. Circle the -ed or -ing word that is spelled correctly.

1.	hop	hoping	hopeing	hopping
2.	bat	batted	bated	bateed
3.	skate	skating	skatting	skateing
4.	bike	bikked	biked	bikeed
5.	hug	huging	hugging	hugiing
6.	wave	waved	waveed	wavvd

Name ________________________________

Words to Know

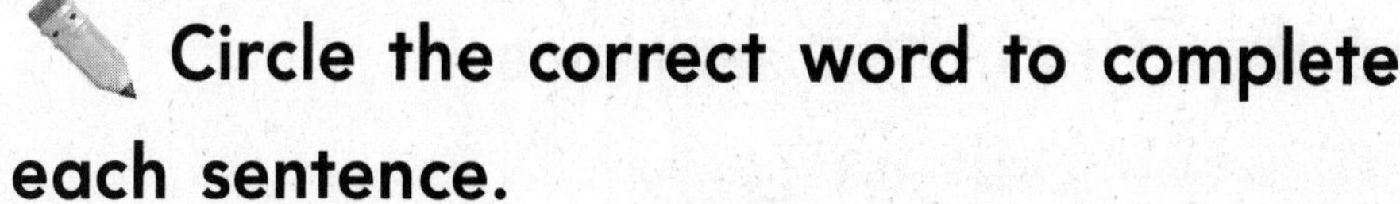

Circle the correct word to complete each sentence.

1. A (even, teacher) helps you learn.

2. Please push that box (toward, pushed) me.

3. A (bear, surprised) is a big animal.

4. The lamp is (above, pushed) the shelf.

5. Mom (teacher, pushed) Kim on the swing.

6. Jim was (surprised, even) by his birthday gift.

7. All the family came, (even, above) Grandma.

8. Ben (toward, studied) the painting closely.

Name ______________________________

Adding *-ed*, *-ing*

Circle the word that fits in the sentence.

1. The cowboy ____________________ a cow.

ropped **roped**

2. A clown was ____________________ a red flag.

waveing **waving**

3. The bull ____________________ running.

stoped **stopped**

4. Kate ____________________ Silver.

peted **petted**

Name ______________________________

Spelling Words Ending in *-ed*, *-ing*

Spelling Words

mix
mixed
hop
hopped
hope
hoping
run
running
use
used

Write the Spelling Words that end in -ing.

1. ______________ 2. ______________

Write the Spelling Words that end in -ed.

3. ______________ 4. ______________

5. ______________

Write the Spelling Words that are base words.

6. ______________ 7. ______________

8. ______________ 9. ______________

10. ______________

Name ____________________

What Is an Exclamation?

 **Draw a line under each exclamation.**

1. The art show was great!

   I saw many paintings.

2. Did you see the painting of the dog?

   I liked that one the most!

3. Dee and Jan put the show together.

   They did a good job!

4. I hope our class can see that show!

   Don't you think so, too?

5. Kay saw the show yesterday.

   She wants to see it again!

Name ______________________

Showing Strong Feelings

Finish these sentences that tell your opinion about Vashti's teacher. Write one exclamation that shows a strong feeling.

Topic Sentence

I think Vashti's teacher is ______________________

____

Detail Sentence

I think so because ______________________

____

Detail Sentence

I also think so because ______________________

____

Name ___________________________

The Dot
Phonics: Long *e* Spelling Patterns *y, ie*

Words with Long *e* Spelling Patterns *y, ie*

Circle the word that matches the picture. Write the word.

1.

bus bunny

2.

park party

3.

baby babies

4.

chief cheese

5.

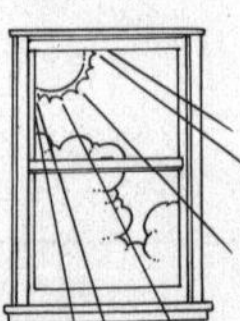

sunny seed

6.

when windy

Name ______________________ Date ______

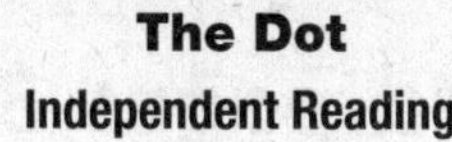

The Dot

Art Awards

Art shows often have awards. The awards are given to the best pieces of art.

Read pages 15–29. Here is an award for the best artwork at the art show.

Which artwork do you think won this award?

____

Why did it win the award?

____

Name ________________________ Date ______

Read pages 30–33. Draw what you think the boy's next artwork will look like. Make an award for it.

Why did it win this award?

Name ______________________________

The Dot
Spelling: Words Ending in *-ed*, *-ing*

Spelling Words Ending in *-ed*, *-ing*

Spelling Words

- mix
- mixed
- hop
- hopped
- hope
- hoping
- run
- running
- use
- used

Add **-ed** to each base word. Then write the new Spelling Word on the line.

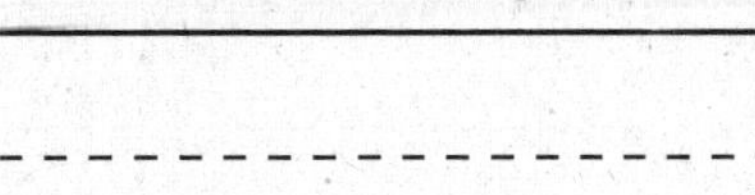

1. mix ______________________

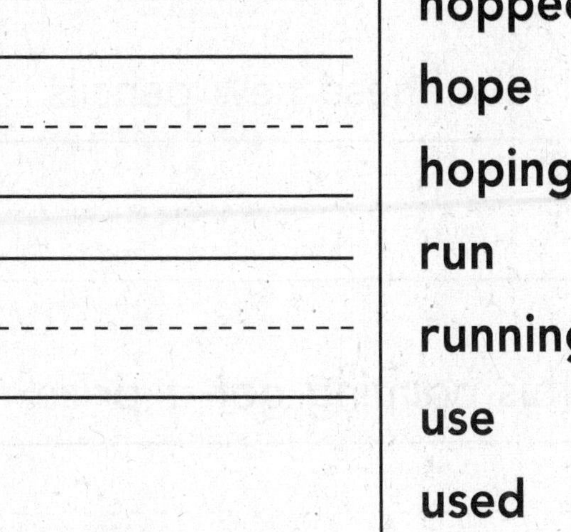

2. hop ______________________

3. use ______________________

Add **-ing** to each base word. Then write the new Spelling Word on the line.

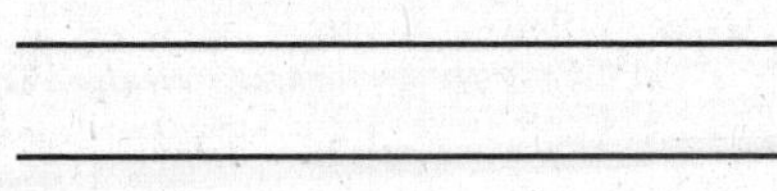

4. hope ______________________

5. run ______________________

Name ____________________

Writing Exclamations

Write each sentence as an exclamation. Begin and end the sentences correctly.

1. those paints are pretty

2. i love these new pencils

3. this painting got a prize

4. there is too much paper

5. we can't wait to draw

Name ______________________________

Planning My Sentences

The Dot
Writing: Opinion Writing

Write your opinion. Then write reasons that tell why. Include a closing sentence.

My Opinion

First Reason

Second Reason

Closing Sentence

Name ______________________

Words with Endings *-ed* and *-ing*

Write the Spelling Word to complete each sentence.

1. The bunny ______________ away.
(hop, hopped)

2. I ______________ I will win the race.
(hope, hoping)

3. He is ______________ very fast.
(run, running)

4. Kim ______________ all the glue in her art project.
(use, used)

5. I ______________ the eggs and the butter.
(mix, mixed)

Name ______________________________

Spiral Review

Circle the pronoun that can take the place of the underlined word or words.

1. Jack and Fred want to paint.

   We **They** **He**

2. Roy drew a picture of a puppy.

   It **He** **She**

3. The picture is very big.

   We **It** **He**

Write He, She, It, We, or They to take the place of the underlined word or words.

4. Jenny went to the art store. ____________

5. Rob and Liz were there. ____________

6. The store is a fun place. ____________

Name ______________________

Grammar in Writing

An **exclamation** is a sentence that shows strong feeling. It ends with an exclamation point (!).

Example: Meg is an artist.

Revised: Meg is the best artist I know!

Revise each sentence. Make it an exclamation.

1. I like blue.

____

2. Mandy drew a picture.

____

3. Karl likes to paint.

____

4. Your pictures are nice.

____

Name ____________________

What Can You Do?
Phonics: Adding *-er*, *-est* (change *y* to *i*)

Adding *-er*, *-est* (change *y* to *i*)

Read the words. Circle the word that does not belong.

1. fancy	fancier	fanciest	find	
2. happy	happier	hand	happiest	
3. silly	sillier	silliest	still	
4. funny	far	funnier	funniest	
5. jolly	jollier	jolliest	joke	
6. messy	miss	messier	messiest	

Name ___________________________

Words to Know

Circle the best answer to each question.

1. What word goes with **far**?	**near**	**high**
2. What word goes with **plot**?	**always**	**stories**
3. What word goes with **when**?	**different**	**once**
4. What word goes with **just right**?	**enough**	**near**
5. What word goes with **low**?	**high**	**happy**
6. What word goes with **sad**?	**once**	**happy**
7. What word goes with **never**?	**high**	**always**
8. What word goes with **same**?	**different**	**stories**

Name ______________________________

What Can You Do?
Phonics: Adding *-er*, *-est* (change *y* to *i*)

Adding *-er*, *-est* (change *y* to *i*)

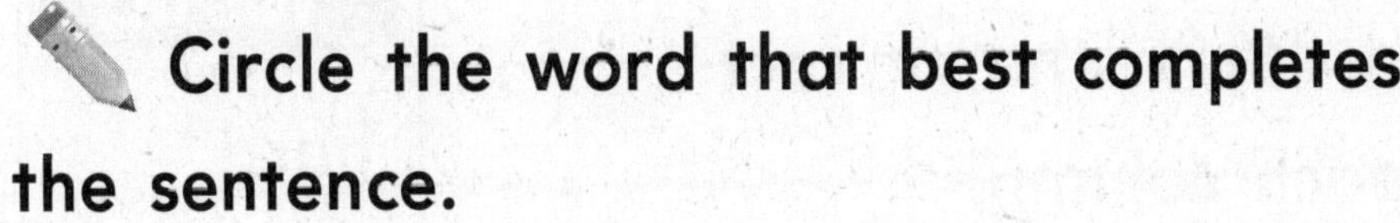

Circle the word that best completes the sentence.

1. My glue is ______ .

sticky **stickier**

2. That chick is the ______ of all.

fluffy **fluffiest**

3. This cupcake is ______ .

yummy **yummiest**

4. My hat is the ______ of all.

fancier **fanciest**

5. Her bird makes the ______ sounds.

sillier **silliest**

6. Luke tells ______ jokes.

funny **funnier**

Name ______________________________

Spelling Words Ending in *-er*, *-est*

What Can You Do?
Spelling: Words Ending in *-er, -est*

Sort the words. Write the correct Spelling Words in each column.

Words with -er	Words with -est

Base Words

Spelling Words

- hard
- harder
- hardest
- fast
- faster
- fastest
- slow
- slower
- slowest
- sooner

Name ______________________________

Question, Exclamation, Statement, or Command?

Draw a line from each question to the question mark (?). Draw a line from each exclamation to the exclamation point (!). Draw a line from each statement or command to the period(.).

1. I really love to sing

?

!

2. Do you play drums

?

!

3. Give the children a snack

?

.

4. Mark makes the snacks

?

.

5. May I have one

?

.

Name ____________________

What Can You Do?
Writing: Opinion Writing

Write Sentences with *Because*

Finish these sentences that tell your opinion about learning something new.

Topic Sentence

Learning to ____________ is ____________.

hard easy

Detail Sentence

One reason is ____________________.

Detail Sentence

Another reason is ____________________.

Closing Sentence

Learning to ____________ is ____________.

Name ____________________

Syllable *-le*

What Can You Do?
Phonics: Syllable *-le*

Circle the word that names the picture.

1.

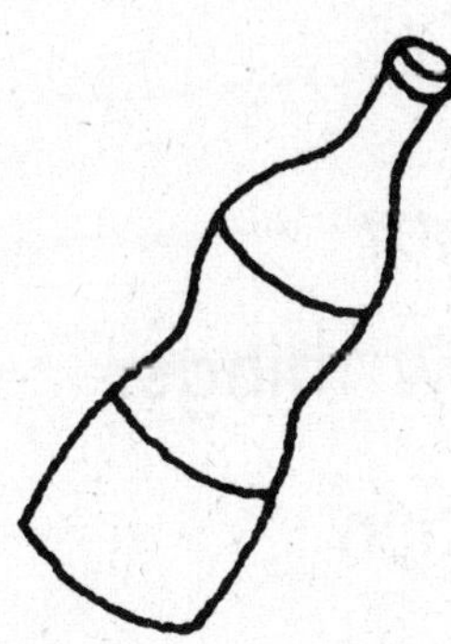

bottle bubble

2.

handle candle

3.

paddle apple

4.

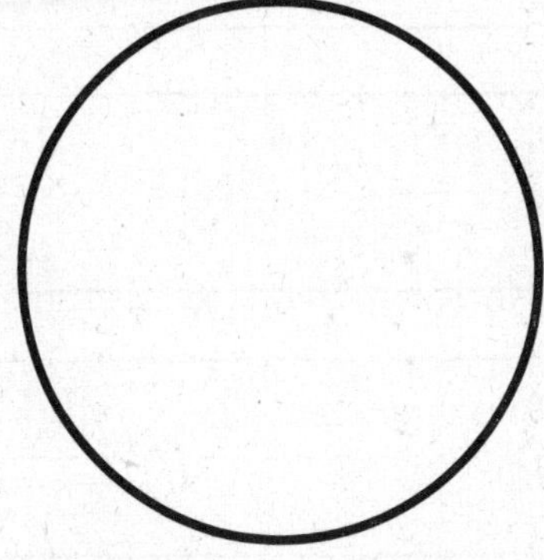

circle cattle

5.

bumble beetle

6.

poodle puzzle

What Can You Do?

Lessons to Learn

The selection has important lessons about practicing, trying hard, and learning new things.

Read pages 51–59. What did you learn about practicing?

Read pages 60–69. What is the moral or lesson of the whole selection?

Name ______________________ Date ______

Think of two animal characters who have a problem they can fix by practicing. List the characters and the setting. Tell what happens first, next, and last. Then write your story on another sheet of paper.

My Characters	My Setting

Events in My Story

Name ______________________

What Can You Do?
Spelling: Words ending in *-er, -est*

Spelling Words Ending in *-er*, *-est*

Spelling Words

- hard
- harder
- hardest
- fast
- faster
- fastest
- slow
- slower
- slowest
- sooner

Add -er to each base word. Then write the new Spelling Word on the line.

1. hard ______________
2. fast ______________
3. slow ______________
4. soon ______________

Add -est to each base word. Then write the Spelling Word on the line.

5. hard ______________
6. fast ______________
7. slow ______________

Name ______________________________

Kinds of Sentences

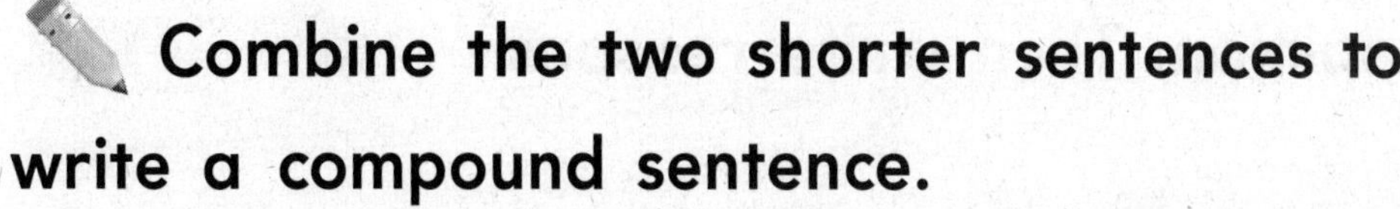

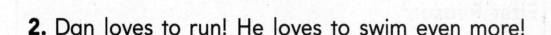

Combine the two shorter sentences to write a compound sentence.

1. Go home. Come with us.

______________________________, or ______________________________

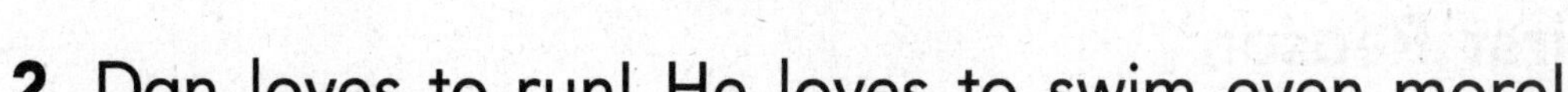

2. Dan loves to run! He loves to swim even more!

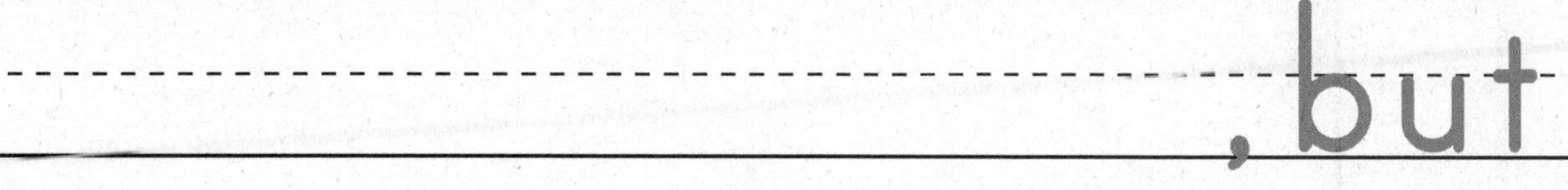

______________________________, but

____

3. I can knit. I can sew.

______________________________, and ______________________________

4. Will Jen come home soon? Will she be out late?

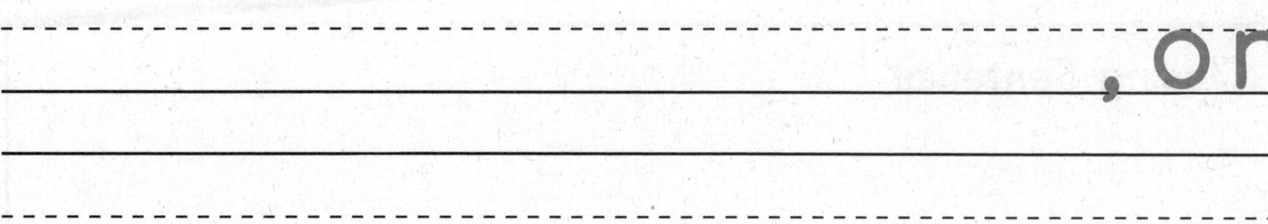

______________________________, or

____

Name ____________________

What Can You Do?
Writing: Opinion Writing

Planning My Sentences

Write your opinion. Then write reasons that tell why.

My Opinion

First Reason

Second Reason

Closing Sentence

Name ______________________

Words with Endings *-er* and *-est*

What Can You Do?
Spelling: Words with *-er* and *-est*

Write the Spelling Word that completes each sentence.

fast **faster** **fastest**

1. The bus goes ______________ .

2. The truck goes ______________ than the bus.

3. The car goes the ______________ .

slow **slower** **slowest**

4. The bug is ______________ .

5. The worm is ______________ than the bug.

6. The turtle is the ______________ of all.

Name ______________________

Spiral Review

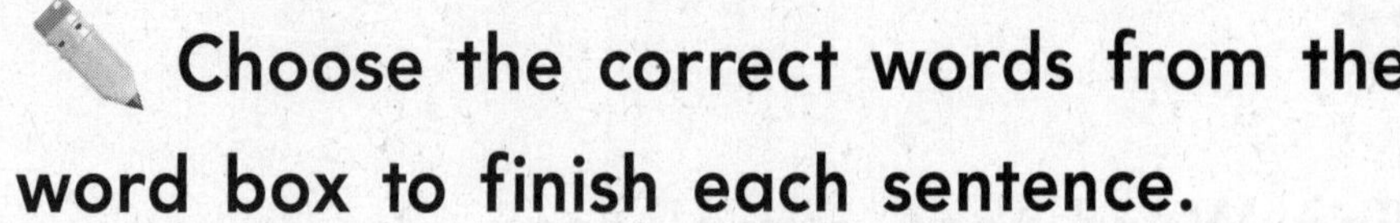

Choose the correct words from the word box to finish each sentence.

Mark	I	me

1. ________ and ________ act in a play.

I	Tammy	me

2. The teacher reads ________ and ________ a story.

me	I	Ricky

3. Nana watches ________ and ________ .

I	me	Sue

4. ________ and ________ like to slide.

Name ________________________________

Grammar in Writing

What Can You Do?
Grammar: Kinds of Sentences

A **statement** and a **command** end with a period. A **question** ends with a question mark. An **exclamation** ends with an exclamation point. All sentences begin with capital letters.

Revise each sentence. Change it to the kind shown in ( ).

Example: Glen can read. (question)
Can Glen read?

1. Is skating fun? (statement)

____

2. I like to ride my bike. (exclamation)

____

3. Chuck likes to act. (question)

____

4. You write a story. (command)

____

Name ________________________________

The Kite
Phonics: Long *i* Spelling Patterns *igh, y, ie*

Long *i* Spelling Patterns *igh*, *y*, *ie*

Look at the picture. Circle the word that names the picture.

1.  spy line

2.  pine pie

3.  sky nine

4.  high hive

5. 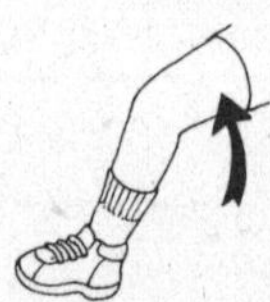 think thigh

6.  fine fly

Name ____________________

Words to Know

Circle the correct word in each sentence.

1. The cat plays with a (ball, head) of yarn.

2. We all (cried, heard) the crash.

3. You (heard, should) try these grapes.

4. Jean is the (second, ball) girl in line.

5. "Let's go!" (cried, heard) Kenny.

6. My (large, head) hurts.

7. We are running (second, across) the field.

8. There is a (large, heard) bird in the tree.

Name ______________________

Long *i* Spelling Patterns *igh, y, ie*

 **Write a word from the box to finish each sentence.**

thigh	dry	try	tie	high

1. Sam hurt his ______________ when he fell.

2. Dad's ______________ has dots and stripes.

3. I will ______________ to swim.

4. The bird will fly up ______________.

5. The wet shirt will ______________.

Name ____________________

Spelling Words with Patterns *igh*, *y*, *ie*

Spelling Words

- my
- try
- sky
- fly
- by
- dry
- pie
- cried
- night
- light

Write the Spelling Words with the igh pattern.

1. ____________________ 2. ____________________

Write the Spelling Words with the ie pattern.

3. ____________________ 4. ____________________

Write the Spelling Words with the y spelling.

5. ____________________ 6. ____________________

7. ____________________ 8. ____________________

9. ____________________ 10. ____________________

Name ____________________

Adjectives for Taste and Smell

Draw a line under each adjective. Then write the adjective.

1. I smell the sweet roses.

2. We taste the bitter lemon.

3. Does the milk smell sour?

Draw a line under each adjective and add commas where they are needed.

4. Some nuts are crunchy sweet and salty.

5. The fruit was sweet moist and chewy.

Name ________________________________

Lesson 28
READER'S NOTEBOOK

The Kite
Writing: Opinion Writing

Using Different Words

Change a repeated word to an exact word. Use a word from the box or your own.

bright	down	high
flew	funny	blue
mean	ran	sunny

Toad went fast, and the kite went up.

Toad ________________ fast, and the kite went up.

The little birds laughed at Toad's little kite.

The little birds laughed at Toad's ________________ kite.

The pretty kite danced in the pretty sky.

The pretty kite danced in the ________________ sky.

Name ____________________

Adding *-ed*, *-ing*, *-er*, *-est*, *-es*

Write the word that best completes each sentence. Use words from the box.

smaller	jumped	riding	highest	foxes

1. Those trees are the ____________ of all.

2. That bird is ____________ than this one.

3. Who is ____________ a red bike?

4. A frog ____________ into the pond.

5. Five ____________ ran to the woods.

Name ______________________ Date ______

Reader's Guide

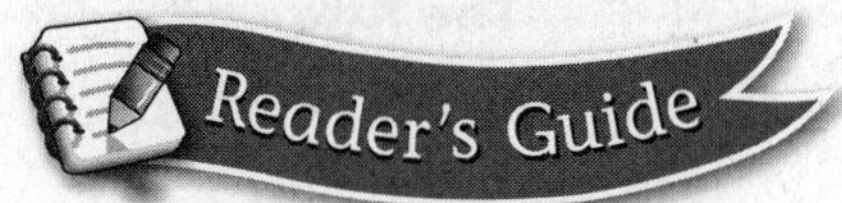

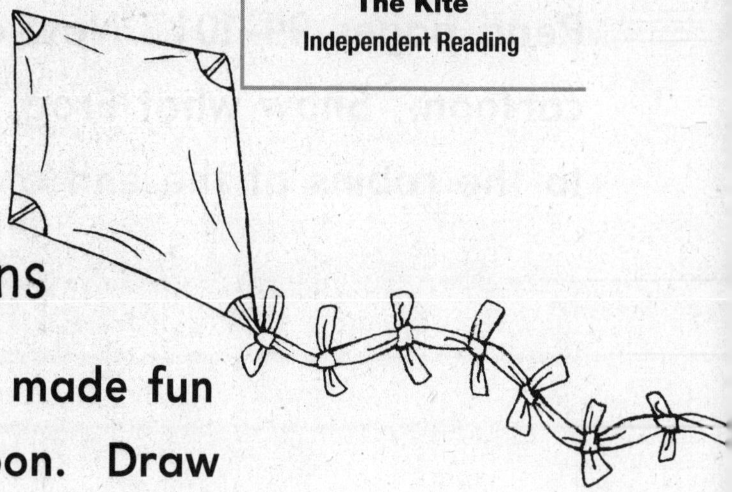

The Kite

Frog, Toad, and the Robins

Read pages 88–93. The robins made fun of the kite. Now draw a cartoon. Draw Frog. Make a speech bubble to show what he says to the robins.

Name ______________________ Date ______

Read pages 94–101. Now draw a cartoon. Show what Frog might say to the robins at the end of the story.

Name ______________________________

Spelling Words with Patterns *igh*, *y*, *ie*

Write each group of Spelling Words in ABC order.

my try sky fly by	dry pie cried night light
______	______
______	______
______	______
______	______
______	______

Spelling Words

my
try
sky
fly
by
dry
pie
cried
night
light

Name ____________________

Adjectives for Sound and Texture

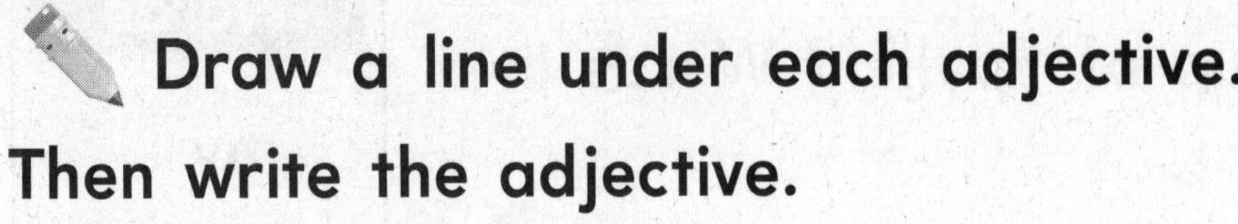

Draw a line under each adjective. Then write the adjective.

1. We sail on the smooth lake.

____

2. I hear the loud cry of a seagull.

____

3. The blanket feels warm.

____

Draw a line under each adjective and add commas where they are needed.

4. The beat was noisy loud and pounding.

5. The music was soft catchy and nice.

Name ______________________________

Planning My Sentences

The Kite
Writing: Opinion Writing

Write your opinion. Then write reasons that tell why. Include a closing sentence.

My Opinion

First Reason

Second Reason

Closing Sentence

Name ______________________________

Spelling Words with *igh*, *y*, *ie*

Write the correct word to complete each sentence.

1. Please turn on the ______________.
(cried, light, pie)

2. Have you seen ______________ book?
(my, try, night)

3. The baby ______________ in her crib.
(fly, dry, cried)

4. Make sure to ______________ the dishes.
(dry, my, light)

5. We went to a great play last ______________.
(light, night, fly)

Name ______________________

Spiral Review

Write the correct pronoun to finish each sentence.

1. Is the yellow kite ______________ ?

   your **yours**

2. That is ______________ kite.

   her **hers**

3. Rex put away ______________ kite.

   he **his**

4. Would you like to play at ______________ house?

   my **mine**

5. We went to ______________ party.

   their **theirs**

Name ______________________________

Grammar in Writing

The Kite
Grammar: Kinds of Adjectives

Some adjectives describe nouns by telling about **taste**, **smell**, **sound**, or **feel**.

Example: I feel the ^cool breeze.

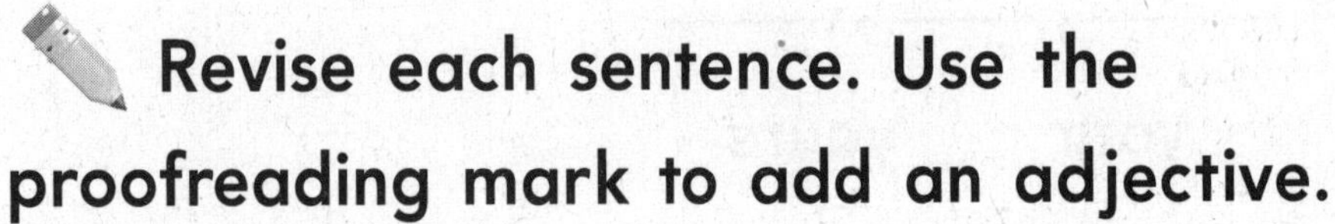

Revise each sentence. Use the proofreading mark to add an adjective.

sweet	fresh	happy	soft

1. Mr. Bee shares some honey.

2. The frog gave a croak.

3. We sit on the grass.

4. We enjoy the air.

Proofreading Mark	
^	add

Name ______________________

Lesson 29
READER'S NOTEBOOK

Hi! Fly Guy
Phonics: Words with Suffixes *-ful, -ly, -y*

Suffixes *-ful*, *-ly*, *-y*

Write a suffix from the box to finish the word.

ful ly y

1.

sad ______

2.

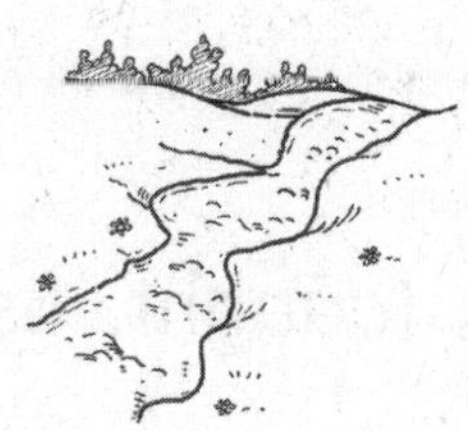

bump ______

3.

dust ______

4.

help ______

5.

slow ______

6.

safe ______

Name ______________________________

Hi! Fly Guy
High-Frequency Words

Words to Know

Circle the correct word to complete each sentence.

1. Planting vegetables is a good (minute, idea).

2. Juan (caught, listen) the ball.

3. Mom (took, caught) us for a haircut.

4. Nancy (idea, thought) about what to bake.

5. My sister has a (beautiful, friendship) new bike.

6. Please (listen, took) to the teacher.

7. My cousin will be here in a (minute, listen).

8. My (beautiful, friendship) with Rita is important to me.

Name ______________________________

Suffixes *-ful*, *-ly*, *-y*

Choose a word from the box. Choose a suffix to make a new word. Write the new word below the suffix.

spoon	snow	sad	trick	
joy	quick	peace	dirt	glad

y	ly	ful
______	______	______
______	______	______
______	______	______

Name ______________________________

Hi! Fly Guy
Spelling: Words with *-ly*, *-y*, *-ful*

Spelling Words with the Suffixes *-ly, -y, -ful*

Spelling Words

- sad
- sadly
- slow
- slowly
- dust
- dusty
- trick
- tricky
- help
- helpful

Write the Spelling Words with -ly.

1. ______________ 2. ______________

Write the Spelling Words with -y.

3. ______________ 4. ______________

Write the Spelling Word with -ful.

5. ______________

Write the Spelling Words that are base words.

6. ______________ 7. ______________

8. ______________ 9. ______________

10. ______________

Name ____________________

Adverbs for How and Where

Circle the adverb in each sentence. Write it on the line.

1. The man went upstairs. ____________

2. The dog followed him closely. ____________

3. Buzz is here. ____________

4. He watched the fly carefully. ____________

Complete each sentence. Write an adverb that tells how or where.

5. The leaf floated ____________ down the stream.

6. Jose stores his new boat ____________.

Name ______________________________

Giving Examples

Look at the picture of the judges on page 139 of your book. Write your opinion about how the judges are feeling about their decision.

I think the judges are feeling ______________.

Write one reason to explain your opinion.

One reason is ______________________________

Write two examples to explain your reason.

1. ______________________________

2. ______________________________

Name ____________________

Long Vowel Spelling Patterns *a, e, i, o, u*

Circle the two words in each row that rhyme. Then write the letter that spells the long vowel sound.

1. table hi fable me ______

2. hi she he go ______

3. kind no flu mind ______

4. flu Stu so be ______

5. we hold wind told ______

Name ______________________ Date ______

Hi! Fly Guy

Fly Talk

You have a special machine.
It tells you what Fly says!

Read pages 119–125. Use your imagination! What does Fly Guy mean when he says "Buzz!" on page 124?

Buzz! →

____

____

____

Read pages 126–128. What does Fly Guy mean when he says "Buzz!" on page 128?

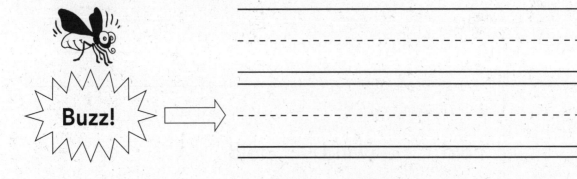

Name ______________________ Date ______

Read pages 129–130. What does Fly Guy mean when he says "Buzz!" on page 130?

Buzz!

Read pages 131–141. What does Fly Guy mean when he says "Buzz!" on page 136?

Name ______________________________

Spelling Words with the Suffixes *-ly, -y, -ful*

Spelling Words

- sad
- sadly
- slow
- slowly
- dust
- dusty
- trick
- tricky
- help
- helpful

Add -ly to each base word. Then write the new Spelling Word on the line.

1. sad ______________________

2. slow ______________________

Add -y to each base word. Then write the new Spelling Word on the line.

3. dust ______________________

4. trick ______________________

Add -ful to the base word. Then write the new Spelling Word on the line.

5. help ______________________

Name ____________________

Adverbs for When and How Much

Circle the adverb in each sentence. Write it on the line.

1. The wagon is too heavy to pull. ____________

2. Dwayne arrived late to the picnic. ____________

3. He was very happy to see his friends. ____________

4. They will have a ball game soon. ____________

Complete each sentence. Write an adverb that tells when or how much.

5. We will have a pet show ____________.

6. The bucket was ____________ full.

Name ______________________________

Words with the Suffixes *-ly*, *-y*, *-ful*

Write the correct word from the box to complete each sentence.

1. I did a card ______________. (trick / tricky)

2. It was ______________ to find the way to the park. (trick / tricky)

3. I like to ______________ wash the car. (help / helpful)

4. When I wash the car, I am very ______________. (help / helpful)

5. I was ______________ to hear my mom call me home. (sad / sadly)

6. I ______________ walked home. (sad / sadly)

Name ____________________

Spiral Review

Indefinite pronouns stand for the names of people or things. They do not take the place of a noun for a certain person or thing, though.

Write the indefinite pronoun that best completes the sentence.

1. Fly Guy knew ____________________ about being a pet.

   something anyone

2. Buzz liked ____________________ about Fly Guy.

   everyone everything

3. ____________________ was amazed by Fly Guy.

   Everyone Everything

4. Did ____________________ teach Fly Guy his tricks?

   everything someone

Name ________________________________

Hi! Fly Guy
Writing: Opinion Writing

Planning My Opinion Paragraph

Write your opinion. Write reasons and examples. Then write a closing sentence.

My Opinion

First Reason

Example

Second Reason

Example

Closing Sentence

Name ___________________________

Grammar in Writing

Adverbs can tell **how**, **where**, **when**, or **how much**.

Examples:	Buzz ran quickly.	how
	Buzz ran here.	where
	Buzz ran yesterday.	when
	Buzz ran a lot.	how much

Rewrite each sentence. Add the kind of adverb shown in ( ).

1. Flies find food. (where)

2. Fly Guy chewed a leaf. (when)

3. He chewed. (how)

4. He ate. (how much)

Name ______________________________

Syllable Pattern CV

Read each word. Draw a line to divide the CV word into two syllables.

1.

music might

2.

baby bone

3.

lace lady

4.

part pilot

5.

robber robot

6.

motel miss

Name ______________________________

Words to Know

Circle the best answer to each clue.

1. This means **all people.**	**everyone**	**field**
2. This means **liked a lot.**	**most**	**loved**
3. These are children and adults.	**sorry**	**people**
4. **Sisters** is its opposite.	**brothers**	**loved**
5. This is a place to play soccer.	**most**	**field**
6. This means **almost all.**	**people**	**most**
7. This means **a certain number.**	**field**	**only**
8. This is a **kind of feeling.**	**sorry**	**everyone**

Name ____________________

Syllable Pattern CV

In each sentence, circle the CV word that has two syllables.

1. It is a bright, shiny day!
2. There is a huge hotel by the lake.
3. Big boats sail in the wavy tide.
4. I hope you decide to come see me.
5. We could take a slow, lazy ride on a boat.

Name ___________________________

Spelling Words with CV Syllables

Spelling Words

- even
- open
- begin
- baby
- tiger
- music
- paper
- zero
- table
- below

Write the Spelling Words with the long e sound in the first syllable.

1. ____________ 2. ____________

3. ____________ 4. ____________

Write the Spelling Words with the long a sound in the first syllable.

5. ____________ 6. ____________

7. ____________

Write the Spelling Words with these long vowel sounds in the first syllable.

8. long **i** ____________ 9. long **o** ____________

10. long **u** ____________

Name ________________

Adjectives with *er* and *est*

Circle the correct adjective to finish each sentence. Write the adjective.

1. Tim is ________________ than Max.

taller **tallest**

2. Fred is the ________________ of them all.

taller **tallest**

3. Cathy is ________________ than Cam.

older **oldest**

4. Adam is the ________________ player of all.

smaller **smallest**

Name ______________________________

Writing a Closing Sentence

Do you think Mia should have quit? Write your own words that explain your opinion. Listen to the words in the Word Bank. Read along. Be sure your last sentence retells your opinion.

Word Bank

agree disagree decision reason example

____

I ______________________________ with Mia's decision to ______________________________

quit. One reason is ______________________________.

____

For example, ______________________________.

____

Another reason is ______________________________.

____

I think ______________________________.

Name ______________________________

Prefixes *un-*, *re-*

Read each word. Circle the word in each box that matches the picture.

1.	2.

untie tried	read repaint
3.	**4.**

setting remove	bedding unbraid
5.	**6.**

untidy neat	unzip unbutton

Name ______________________ Date ______

Winners Never Quit!

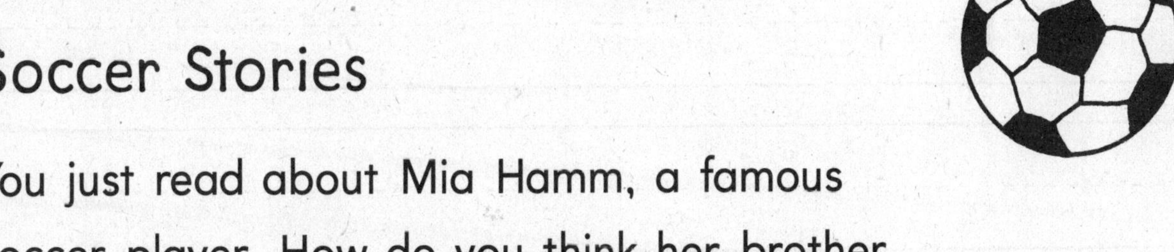

Soccer Stories

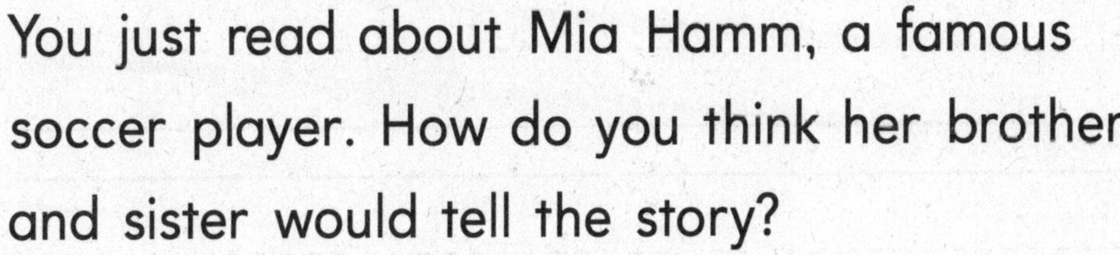

You just read about Mia Hamm, a famous soccer player. How do you think her brother and sister would tell the story?

Read pages 159–167. How do you think Lovdy would tell this part of the story?

Name ______________________ Date ______

Winners Never Quit!
Independent Reading

Read pages 168–177. How do you think Garrett would tell this part of the story?

Do you think Mia scored at the end? What do you think Lovdy and Garrett said to her?

Name ______________________________

Spelling Words with CV Syllables

Write the Spelling Word that fits each clue.

Spelling Words

- even
- open
- begin
- baby
- tiger
- music
- paper
- zero
- table
- below

1. Opposite of **closed** ______________

2. A very young person ______________

3. Something to listen to ______________

4. Opposite of **end** ______________

5. Opposite of **above** ______________

6. An animal ______________

Name ______________________

Using the Right Adjective

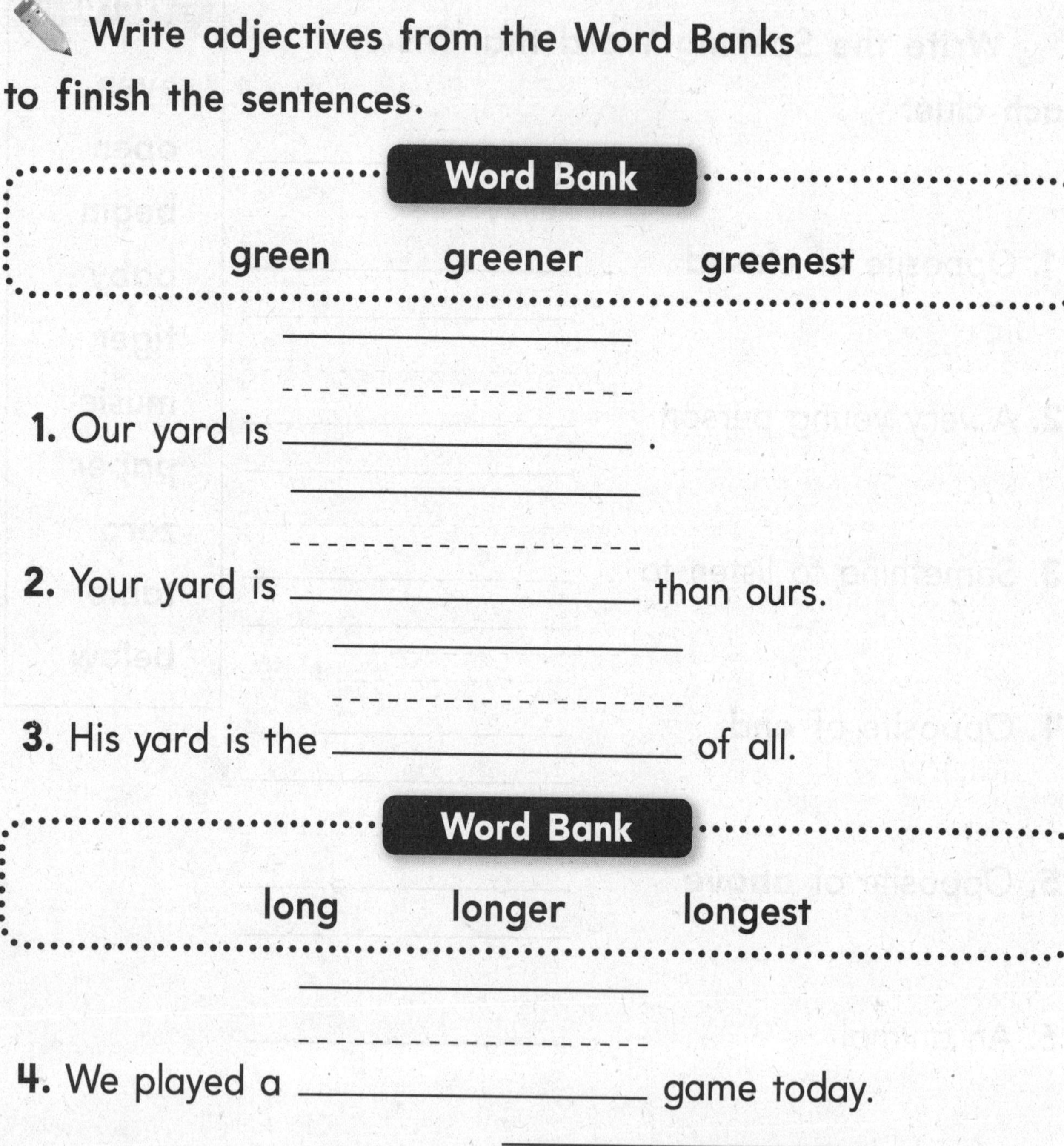

Write adjectives from the Word Banks to finish the sentences.

Word Bank

green greener greenest

1. Our yard is ______________ .

2. Your yard is ______________ than ours.

3. His yard is the ______________ of all.

Word Bank

long longer longest

4. We played a ______________ game today.

5. The game yesterday was ______________ than the game today.

Name ______________________________

Spelling Words with Syllable Pattern CV

Write the correct word to complete each sentence.

1. Ken saw a ______________ at the zoo. (below, tiger)

2. Please sit and ______________ your test. (even, begin)

3. What kind of ______________ do you like? (below, music)

4. I used red ______________ to make the card. (paper, zero)

5. The food is on the ______________ . (open, table)

Name ________________

Spiral Review

Choose contractions from the box for the underlined words. Write the contractions.

Word Bank

He's
I'm
can't
They're
isn't

1. They are tennis players.

2. I cannot wait to play with her.

3. It is not hard to play.

4. He is learning now!

5. I am having fun.

Name ______________________________

Grammar in Writing

- Add **er** to adjectives to compare two.
- Add **est** to compare more than two.

Example: Today is warm.

Today is the warmest day of the summer.

Revise each sentence. Use an adjective that compares. Add other words, too.

1. Beth is a fast runner.

____

2. Tad is tall.

____

3. Our team is stronger.

____

4. Today was cold.

____

Name ________________________________ Date ______

Owl at Home

Case of the Messy Houseguest

Read pages 5–17. Owl thinks Winter came into his house and made a big mess. Is he right?

Write in the detective journal. What do you think really happened? Use clues from the text and pictures to explain your answer.

Name ______________________________ Date ______

Case of the Mysterious Bumps

Read pages 19–29. There are two bumps at the bottom of Owl's bed. What are they?

Use your detective skills to solve the mystery! Write what you think the bumps are. Use clues from the text and pictures to explain your answer.

Name ______________________ Date ______

Owl at Home

Case of the Tear-Water Tea

Read pages 31–39. Owl makes salty tea. Why is the tea salty?

Write in the detective journal. Tell why the tea is salty. Use clues from the text and pictures to explain your answer.

Name ______________________ Date ______

Case of the Upstairs and Downstairs

Read pages 41–49. Help Owl understand why he cannot be upstairs and downstairs at the same time.

Use clues from the story to explain. Draw a picture and label it to solve the mystery for Owl.

Owl at Home

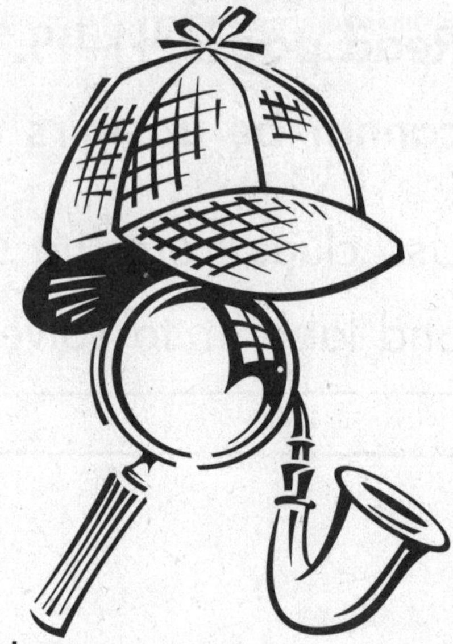

Case of the Moon Friend

Read pages 51–64. Owl looks at the moon and thinks it is a friend. Can the moon be Owl's friend?

Write your answer. Use clues from the text and pictures to explain.

Name ______________________ Date ______

Meet Owl

Use what you know about Owl to help him build a webpage. First, draw a picture of Owl in the box. Then fill in the blanks.

My Name: ______________________

I live in ______________________.

My favorite place is ______________________.

My favorite drink is ______________________.

My favorite thing to do is ______________________.

Right now, you can find me ______________________.

Reading and Writing Glossary

Use this glossary to help you remember and use words that you are learning about reading and writing.

A

adjective A word that describes a person, an animal, a place, or a thing. An adjective may tell how something looks, tastes, smells, sounds, or feels.

adverb A word that describes a verb. An adverb may tell how, where, when, or how much something is. An adverb may end in *-ly*.

alphabetical order When words are listed in the same order as letters of the alphabet.

antonym A word that means the opposite or nearly the opposite of another word.

apostrophe A punctuation mark (') that takes the place of missing letters in a word.

article A special word, such as *a*, *an*, or *the*, that comes before a noun.

author A person who writes a story.

author's purpose The reason why an author writes a text.

B

base word A word to which beginning and ending word parts can be added. A base word is also known as a root word.

biography Informational text that tells about events in a real person's life.

C

caption Words that tell about a picture or a photograph.

categorize To name a group of similar things.

category A group of like objects or things.

cause The reason why something happens in a story or text.

chapter book A story that is divided into parts.

characteristic A special quality or trait.

characters The people and animals in a story.

checklist A list of names or things to think about or do.

classify To place similar things in a group.

command A sentence that tells someone to do something. A command can end with a period (.) or an exclamation mark (!).

compare To tell how things are the same.

compound sentence A sentence that is made up of two shorter sentences. The parts of a compound sentence may be connected by words such as *and*, *or*, and *but*.

conclusion A good guess about something the author does not say.

context The words and sentences around a word or phrase that give readers clues to its meaning.

contraction A short way of writing two words using an apostrophe (').

contrast To tell how things are different.

D

detail A fact that tells more about the main idea.

dialogue What characters say in a story.

E

effect The result of something that happens in a story or text.

entry word A word listed in a dictionary with a definition.

event Something that happens.

exclamation A sentence that shows a strong feeling. An exclamation begins with a capital letter and ends with an exclamation point (!).

F

fable A short story that teaches a lesson.

fairy tale An old story with characters that can do amazing things.

fantasy A type of story that could not happen in real life.

figurative language Words authors use to help a reader picture things in a story. These words may have more than one meaning.

folktale An old story that people have told for many years.

G

glossary A list of words with their definitions, often at the back of a book.

graph A drawing that uses numbers, colors, pictures, or symbols to give information.

graphic features Photos or drawings that stand for ideas or add details in the text.

heading A title for a section of a text.

homograph A word that is spelled the same as another word but has a different meaning and may be pronounced differently.

homophone A word that sounds like another word but is spelled differently and has a different meaning.

I

indefinite pronoun A special pronoun, like *anyone*, *everything*, *someone*, *something*, or *everyone*. An indefinite pronoun does not stand for a certain person or thing.

informational text Text that tells about things that are real and contains facts.

informative writing Writing that gives facts about a topic.

M

main idea The most important idea about the topic.

multiple-meaning word A word with more than one meaning.

N

narrative nonfiction A story that gives information about real people, settings, and events.

narrative writing Writing that tells a story. A narrative tells about something that happened to a person or a character.

narrator The person who tells the story.

noun A word that names a person, an animal, a place, or a thing.

O

onomatopoeia Using words that sound like real noises.

opinion writing Writing that tells what the writer believes and gives reasons.

P

plot The order of events in a story, including the problem and how it is solved.

plural noun A noun that names more than one person, animal, place, or thing. A plural noun usually ends in *-s* or *-es*.

poetry Uses the sounds of words to show pictures and feelings. Poetry sometimes uses rhyming words and other patterns.

possessive noun A noun that shows that one person or animal owns or has something.

possessive pronouns A type of pronoun that shows that something belongs to someone.

predicate The part of a sentence that tells what someone or something does.

prefix A word part attached to the beginning of a base word or root word that changes the word's meaning.

preposition A word that joins with other words to help explain where something is or when it happens.

prepositional phrase A group of words that starts with a preposition.

proper noun A noun that names a special person, animal, place, or thing. A proper noun begins with a capital letter.

---

question A sentence that asks something. A question begins with a capital letter and ends with a question mark (?).

quotation marks Punctuation marks (" ") that go around the words a character says.

R

realistic fiction A made-up story that could happen in real life.

repetition The same words or same kind of event used over and over in a text.

research report Writing that tells what a writer learned from doing research about a topic.

rhythm A pattern of beats in a poem.

S

sentence A group of words that tells a complete idea.

sequence of events The order in which things happen.

setting When and where a story takes place.

simile Words that tell how two things are the same, using *like* or *as*.

singular noun A noun that names one person, animal, place, or thing.

statement A sentence that tells something. A statement begins with a capital letter and ends with a period (.).

story lesson The lesson a story teaches or its main message.

subject The part of a sentence that tells who or what.

subject pronoun A word that can take the place of a subject, such as *he*, *she*, *it*, *we*, or *they*.

suffix One or more letters that are added to the end of a root word to change the word's meaning.

synonym A word that has the same or almost the same meaning as another word.

T

text and graphic features Photographs, labels, headings, captions, illustrations, dark print, and other special features that add information to a text.

text evidence Clues in the words and pictures that help you figure things out.

thesaurus A book of words in alphabetical order with their synonyms.

topic What a text is mostly about.

V

verb A word that tells what people and animals do.

W

word choice Words writers choose to make their writing clear and interesting, such as words that describe how things look, feel, sound, smell, or taste.